The Wise Leader

The Wise Leader offers readers a succinct perspective on wise leadership based on theory, practice, and the authors' own experience.

The five sections of the book describe the Wise Leader model, five mantras that distil the essence of wisdom for leading. Each section has a theoretical component, theory that the authors seek to bring to life through everyday examples, followed by practical ideas and guidance as to what you can next do in service of becoming a wiser, more effective leader. Each mantra then includes fresh perspectives for leadership development, aimed at supporting organizations globally to maximize their considerable investment in this critical area.

This book is written for leaders at every level of an organization, providing a perspective of wise leadership that lends itself to practical application. It can also be used by leadership development professionals, offering guidance on how to build practical programs to cultivate enhanced levels of wise leadership in your organization.

Dr Paul Lawrence enjoyed a long corporate career, leading teams and businesses in the UK, Spain, Portugal, Australia, and Japan. Paul has been working as a coach and consultant since 2007, based in Sydney Australia, and is a research associate at Oxford Brookes University in the UK.

Dr Suzi Skinner combines her global corporate background with her international leadership development practice. Since 2001 Suzi has been integrating evidence-based leadership practices to drive positive culture change with clients worldwide. Based in Sydney Australia, Suzi is a lecturer and research associate at Sydney Business School, University of Wollongong.

The Wise Leader

A Practical Guide for Thinking Differently About Leadership

Paul Lawrence, PhD, and
Suzi Skinner, PhD

Routledge
Taylor & Francis Group
LONDON AND NEW YORK

Designed cover image: Cienpies as rendered the owner on Getty Images.

First published 2024
by Routledge
4 Park Square, Milton Park, Abingdon, Oxon OX14 4RN

and by Routledge
605 Third Avenue, New York, NY 10158

Routledge is an imprint of the Taylor & Francis Group, an informa business

British Library Cataloguing-in-Publication Data
A catalogue record for this book is available from the British Library

ISBN: 978-1-032-25672-6 (hbk)
ISBN: 978-1-032-25749-5 (pbk)
ISBN: 978-1-003-28482-6 (ebk)

DOI: 10.4324/9781003284826

Typeset in Times New Roman
by MPS Limited, Dehradun

To David and Loraine, Sylvia and John, and all parents everywhere

Contents

Introduction

We need to change the way we think about leadership. The traditional approach to leadership is not serving us well and we need to look elsewhere for inspiration. In this book, we look to the world of wisdom to search for insights that will help us become better leaders. Some of the wisdom material feels quite intangible, and so we have married the wisdom literature with psychological perspectives on leadership, perspectives that lend themselves to practical application. In doing so we bring different ways of knowing, being, and seeing to help leaders better dance in the complexity that characterizes our world today.

The psychology of wisdom remains a relatively unexplored area[1]. Dictionary definitions of wisdom make no reference to psychology. From our work bringing the two domains together, we believe we have found a fresh approach to leadership, one that is practical and accessible, no matter what level of leadership you are or aspire to be. We invite you to consider how you can access the wisest parts of yourselves in service of becoming more effective in your role, in your family, or in your community. If you design leadership programs, we invite you to think about how you can best facilitate the emergence of wisdom in others.

The traditional approach

We are forever coming across binary notions of leadership that talk to i) the leader's capacity to work out how to get things done and, ii) their capacity to 'bring people on the journey'. Leaders who are therefore smart and empathetic should be great leaders. We don't think this depiction of leadership is complete. Intelligence and empathy are not enough.

1 Intelligence is important and intelligence is not enough

Many definitions of wisdom talk about our capacity for logical, rational, thinking. This form of intelligence is important, but it is not enough, and it is not the same as wisdom. Many of our leaders have impressive credentials,

DOI: 10.4324/9781003284826-1

multiple university degrees, and high IQs, but still, we watch those leaders make unfathomable decisions. Our collective IQ climbed 30 points in the last 100 years, or 3 points every decade[2]. Yet as we apparently become more intelligent, so we seem to be falling behind in our ability to navigate the issues of the day.

Over a century ago, Frederick Winslow Taylor framed five principles of scientific management[3]. Those principles told organizations to shift responsibility for the organization of work from the worker to the manager. They told management to use scientific methods to design jobs, to train workers to understand what they need to do, and to monitor performance to ensure procedures are followed and results are obtained. Unfortunately, these five principles clearly position the leader as the smartest person in the room. The leader is the one who decides how best to organize the work and then enforces that decision. The primary attributes of such a manager include decisiveness, autonomy, certainty, and – above all – an analytical form of intelligence. But clever leaders are not always wise leaders, and clever leaders often come unstuck.

For example, 30 years ago, Robert Horton took over the reins as CEO and Chairman of BP. His style was brusque and autocratic. He was quoted as saying, '*Because I am blessed by my good brain, I tend to get the answer rather quicker and more often than most people. That will sound frightfully arrogant*'[4]. It does sound frightfully arrogant. In 1992, just two years into the role, Horton was asked to resign because (clever though he was) he made bad decisions. BP then enjoyed a period of growth, first under the stewardship of David Simon and then John Browne. John Browne presided over a period of extraordinary growth achieved through a long series of mergers and acquisitions. In 2002 he was described as the 'Sun King' by the Financial Times, in recognition both of his success and somewhat monarchical stature within BP[5]. Around this time things started to go wrong for BP. The problems started in 2002 when Browne had to restate BP's production targets three times in a row. Browne's reputation was further dented by the Texas City Oil Refinery disaster in 2005 and the Prudhoe Bay oil spill in 2006. Browne said in his autobiography, he wished other executives had stood up against him more, '*I wish someone had challenged me and been brave enough to say: "We need to ask more disagreeable questions"*'[6]. Those other executives were experienced, well-seasoned, professionals. What was it about Browne that discouraged them from challenging him? Browne was a problem solver at heart. He says in the introduction to his autobiography '*I joined BP because I liked solving problems*'. In the same introduction, he writes about how '*I went on to transform BP*', and how '*I transformed a company*', couching those efforts as personal rather than collective achievements. This is the narrative of a clever individual, framing his leadership in terms of intelligence. Intelligence is not enough. Being clever is not enough.

2 Empathy is important and empathy is not enough

To bring people on the journey requires empathy. It requires us to engage with people to understand what motivates them. Winslow Taylor's approach may have resulted in an efficient process, but it also resulted in bored, disengaged workers. In the 1920s and 1930s, Elton Mayo studied workers at the Hawthorne Plant of the Western Electric Company in Chicago[7]. He found they performed at their best only when motivated. Organizational psychologists built on Mayo's work, encouraging leaders to develop their 'soft skills'. Soft skills, as they are conceptualized, are positioned as the skills required to engage and motivate others. In our experience, these skills are anything but 'soft' and are difficult to master. Accordingly, organizations would love these soft skills to be more measurable, and so the idea of EQ has evolved. But not everyone agrees on what EQ is and there are no reliable tests for EQ. Tools such as MSCEIT have multiple flaws[8] but they continue to be used by organizations seeking some means by which to reliably measure and evaluate empathy. Nevertheless, we know empathy is important.

If we could measure empathy then we might have more effective leadership, but we wouldn't necessarily have wise leadership. Neither intelligence nor empathy by themselves talks to motive. People can be highly intelligent and capable of tuning into how other people feel, but also be selfish. Selfishness sits at the heart of many of our troubles. Politicians who value their job security above moral principles. National leaders who seek to protect their economies or extend their boundaries without thought to people living in other countries. Business leaders seek to drive the value of their organizations without thought to the impact of their activities. These people may be clever, and capable of tuning into how other people are feeling, but so often they are not wise.

Wisdom

We believe now is the time to explore wisdom. People are no more aligned around a single definition of wisdom than they are around a single definition of leadership, but some aspects show up more frequently than others. So, we do see attributes such as reasoning ability and good judgment, both of which may relate to intelligence. We also see compassion and empathy. But we see other traits too, such as emotional regulation, life experience, humility, self-awareness, openness to change, propensity to reflect, a positive mindset, comfort with ambiguity, commitment to learning, and a desire to serve the common good. Many of these traits are now starting to show up in more recent theories of outstanding leadership[9].

Reading this list of wise attributes, we may feel tempted to try and convert them into new skills and competencies, and then teach these skills to our leaders in the hope they will become wiser. The traditional approach is unlikely to work, however, because many of these traits talk to the way we *think*. This is where some leaders and leadership development professionals start to feel uncomfortable. They don't want to get into discussions about ideas and theories. To do so would be impractical. They want to know what to *do* differently. This is an example of binary thinking, in our view. To be wise is to think differently. If we want to become wiser then we must make the time to reflect, to think about how we think. But we don't do that for the sake of it. We do it because (as Plato suggested) those who attain wisdom cannot help but practice it[10].

Some writers define wisdom in terms of a desire to serve a common good, and to put others before ourselves. If this is an aspect of wisdom, then how do we turn *that* into a skill or competency? Or is it a personality trait, something we have or have not? Many of us live in highly individualistic societies, societies that value autonomy and independence, societies with little time for the less fortunate – the losers[11]. Buddhism suggests that selfishness is the key obstacle to becoming wise[12]. Robert Sternberg has written extensively about wisdom in terms of balancing our individual needs with the needs of others[13]. Paul Baltes said that the main motivation underlying the development of wisdom is not a striving for excellence, but a desire to improve others' lives[14]. We highlight this aspect of wisdom because it is so difficult to think about as a skill or something we can teach in a classroom. What we believe to be important, our purpose in life, evolves as we grow and develop. We believe leaders can aspire to be wiser in this sense, that they can develop their capacity to view their world through the lens of others. And we believe that leadership development professionals can create environments that facilitate this evolution. As we write this, we wonder what it would be like to work in an organization that was truly focused on the needs of the many. And how we can take purposeful steps to co-create such environments?

We cite the desire to serve a common good as just one aspect of wisdom that doesn't lend itself to framing as a skill or competence. Many aspects of leadership are about who we are being, not so much what we are doing. Who we are being relates to how we are thinking, and if we can shift who we are being and how we are thinking, then we will find ourselves doing things differently. In this book, we offer you a pathway to becoming wiser, not only in terms of serving a common good but more broadly with regard to all those aspects of wisdom that sit beyond intelligence and empathy.

Wisdom and leadership

There is a vast literature on wisdom, with multiple definitions emerging from different cultures[15]. You may have heard of Sophistic civic wisdom, Socratic wisdom, Platonic wisdom, Aristotelian wisdom, and so on. We don't attempt

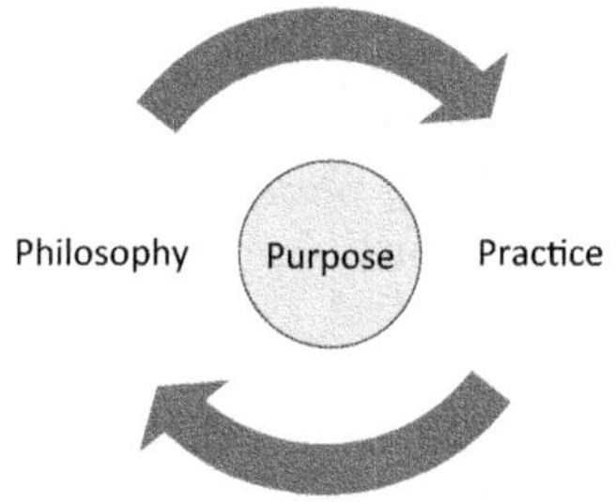

Figure I.1 The 3Ps.

to review all these approaches, nor condense those theories into a single perspective. Instead, we align ourselves with a view that says the way people think about wisdom depends on their particular worldview as it relates to the work that they do[16]. Whether or not we are seen to be wise depends on the views of others in our culture[17]. One might frame the world of leadership as a professional domain, a particular culture, but we think that is too broad a perspective to be useful. We all work in different professional domains and in different cultures, and so in this book, we invite you to create your own personal depiction of wisdom. Your frame must include how you *think* as well as what you *do*, as we have already explained, and your articulation of wisdom must refer to your *purpose*. Researchers have demonstrated explicit relations between wisdom and purpose[18]. Wise leaders are purposeful.

So, as you read this book, we encourage you to begin thinking about your 3Ps of Wise Leadership. The 3Ps will help you reflect on who you are as a leader and who you aspire to become. The 3Ps stand for your Philosophy, Purpose, and Practice as a leader (Figure I.1).

Philosophy

What is your existing philosophy of wise leadership? By this, we mean what are your favourite theories and models as they relate to leading? Why these theories and models? How do they relate to your beliefs, values, and experiences?

Purpose

Why do you lead? You don't *have* to be a leader – why do you do it? What gets you up in the morning? And how do you know if you are achieving your purpose? Notice this is a different question to – what do other people think of you? This is more about what do you think of yourself and your attempts to becoming the leader you want to be.

Practice

How do your philosophies and purpose show up in the way you behave day to day? If we were to follow you around for a day, what would you see yourself doing? What would we not see you doing?

We invite you to make some notes now on who you are as a leader, through the lens of the 3Ps. And as you read the book, we invite you to consider how that construction evolves.

As you begin to ponder on what wise leadership means to you, we invite you to reflect a while on three questions, maybe while making a cup of tea and giving yourself some time to think before reading on to see how others answered these three questions:

1 How many leaders you have worked with in your career would you describe as wise?
2 In the public domain – which leaders do you think are wise?
3 What attributes do you associate with being wise?

We asked these same three questions of 50 leaders in an informal straw poll. In answering the first question, half the respondents said they had never worked with a wise leader. Just two people said they had worked with lots of wise leaders. The average respondent named four leaders.

In answering the second question, again some people said they couldn't think of any wise leaders in the public domain while others listed up to a dozen people. The average response was two leaders. People named leaders from past and present, political leaders, business leaders, military leaders, religious leaders, activists, musicians, actors, writers, sportsmen, and television personalities. Between them, our 50 respondents named 58 different leaders. Only eight people were named more than once: Barack Obama, Jacinda Arden, Volodymyr Zelenskyy, the Dalai Lama, Mahatma Gandhi, Angela Merkel, Pope Francis, and Nelson Mandela.

The 50 respondents listed 88 different adjectives to describe wisdom. The most popular were adjectives relating to thoughtfulness, including the capacity to see the big picture and hold multiple perspectives. They named the capacity of the leader to empathize, to connect, and to engage respectfully with others. They named the extent to which a leader was purposeful, calm, considered, humble, self-aware, ethical, curious, and knowledgeable. And they talked about wisdom in terms of experience and a desire to serve the collective good. Not every respondent named every attribute, and we could see some people leaning more towards being thoughtful and having the capacity to hold multiple perspectives. Others leaned more toward compassion and empathy. Others highlighted the desire of the leader to serve others. Amidst these attributes, we do find judgment and empathy, and we find perspective-taking. In addition, we find purpose, calmness, humility, morality, curiosity, and a desire to serve others. In this book, we look beyond our ad-hoc straw poll and look to the literature on wisdom to see how we might usefully define wisdom and how we might help each other become wiser.

The need for wisdom

Today's world, to many if not most of us, feels increasingly uncertain, volatile, and out of control. Here on the east coast of Australia, we have experienced widespread bushfires, COVID, and flooding in the last couple of years, all in quick succession. These events haven't just hurt the economy, for some, they have been personally catastrophic. An increasing and progressive trend in the frequency of natural disasters means that insurers will no longer insure properties in certain geographies, which leaves some people effectively homeless. Changing weather patterns bring different forms of devastation to different parts of the world. As we write, one-third of Pakistan is underwater, and tens of millions of people are affected. And as the impact of climate change becomes clearer, we hear predictions of whole country populations becoming homeless within the next 30 years. In the meantime, we show little capacity for aligning around a collective response. Some people even deny, still, that climate change is real. We don't like uncertainty and so many of our leaders seek to simplify what they see, to reduce it to something utterly understandable and controllable.

Consider COVID-19. Some people recognized early that COVID-19 was complex and urged us all to work out together how best to manage it. Others were convinced they could control it with existing resources and diminished its significance. These people sought to simplify something complex in service of minimizing anxiety and uncertainty. COVID was likened to influenza because we are familiar with influenza and the prospect of a new strain of influenza is easier to contemplate than a brand new, more serious, virus.

Similarly, when the UK engaged in a debate about whether to remain part of the European Union, we heard leaders reduce the enormous complexity of that decision to simple choices, articulated in the form of slogans such as '*We send the EU £350 million a week. Let's fund the NHS instead.*' These leaders assured people that existing trade deals would be replaced by new trade deals. They assured people that there existed solutions for managing the border between Ireland and Northern Ireland. In short, they sought to simplify something extremely complex because they knew their simpler perspective on the world would assure people that Brexit posed no threat to their standards of living and would enable them to feel more autonomous and independent.

We don't manage these issues well. We can blame our leaders, but we would do well to acknowledge that our leaders are our leaders because we vote them into office (in democratic countries anyway). If we want to be governed by wise leaders, then we must *all* reflect on what we believe to be wise leadership. We can all become wiser, no matter our status in the world. It is up to all of us to make a difference, to challenge our own thinking and behaviours. Our issues are ours to manage, we cannot blame our leaders for everything. We all need to take personal responsibility for how we together approach the challenges we face today. Here *we* are. Alone and together. We must *all* ask ourselves – what impact are we having? What choices are we making? Who are we being? Wisdom is a societal issue.

Wisdom and leadership development

We need to think differently about leadership development. We still see too many leadership development programs constructed around a few key models and theories. The focus is on information download and knowledge transfer. This approach to leadership development typifies the approach of many business schools. The problem with this approach is that students find it difficult to apply the models and theories to their everyday work and the content is soon forgotten[19]. There are some good offerings out there too, so how do we choose between all these different programs, or else develop a framework for building our own? Again, we believe that a useful worldview on leadership development includes how you *think* about leadership as well as what your programs will look like. So, just as we encourage the leader to consider their 3Ps of wise leadership, so we encourage leadership development professionals to consider their 3Ps of wise leadership development.

Philosophy

Many program designers we talk to, talk about the *content* of their program, whether it features tried and trusted models, or the latest popular article/book on leadership. About content – do you have your own clear perspective on leadership? What is leadership to you, and how do all the myriad of books, models, and frameworks shape up against your *leadership philosophy*? We hear less conversation around *process*. What does your program need to look and feel like if you are going to facilitate the emergence of sustainable new behaviours? How much time do you spend researching learning? Are you a learning expert or a project manager? What is your *learning philosophy*?

Purpose

Be purposeful. Robert Sternberg & Emily Hagen suggest that the purpose of an effective wise leadership program is to enable people to become more self-aware, to develop a heightened sense of their own morality, and to enhance their capacity for self-reflection[20]. What is *your* purpose for your organization? How will you know if you are achieving your purpose?

If you run a leadership program these days, you are most probably encouraged to focus on delivering your program cost-effectively and efficiently. You may be encouraged to inflate class sizes on the basis that this delivers a better ROI. It does deliver a better ROI if you measure the R in terms of the number of bodies processed, or the number of people who rate your program as a five-star program. Neither measure is helpful. Consider, what is the purpose of your program and how will you measure the extent to which your offering is delivering on that purpose. There are ways to measure the impact of your program on people's experience of leadership in your organization, in-depth methodologies that enable you to understand what is happening, and how to tweak your programs to be more impactful.

Practice

How do your philosophies and purpose show up in the programs you commission and design? There are many aspects of design, and we will touch on those as we proceed through the rest of the book, but here we will make special mention of group coaching. Here are just a few insights from the world of wisdom that point to the value of group coaching:

- People learn to become wise through social interaction
- People become wiser through reflection
- People become wiser through 'dialogical thinking' – developing the ability to see problems from different perspectives
- Wisdom can be fostered through the use of stories
- People need space to come up with their own answers

Group coaching is a wonderful medium for creating such an environment. A focus on group coaching acknowledges the value of reflecting together. As Sternberg & Hagen say, '*Educators should not be seen as omniscient sources of information, but rather as facilitators of student reflections*'. From our experience, we have learned that effective group coaches see their role as being to facilitate the conversation not to teach new content. People share their own stories, not pre-prepared case studies. They engage with others and learn about themselves and others through those interactions. We do see group coaching used in some of the programs we see, though often program designers can't resist introducing some 'teach'. The people who deliver your leadership programs – how much time do they spend imparting information? How much time do they spend facilitating individual and group reflection? As will become evident as you read on, we believe that the secret sauce in developing wisdom in leaders is the enabling of the kind of powerful learning dynamic that can emerge through group coaching. Effective group coaching allows every voice to be heard and every participant is given space to reflect on the impact of their own ways of thinking on others.

Book structure

In this book we offer you:

1 A succinct perspective on wise leadership based on theory, practice, and our own experience.
2 For leaders, a perspective of wise leadership that lends itself to practical application.
3 For leadership development professionals, guidance on how to build practical programs to cultivate enhanced levels of wise leadership in your organisation.

The five sections of the book describe our Wise Leader model. The Wise Leader model comprises five mantras, five mantras that capture every aspect of wisdom so far described. We connect each mantra to theories of wisdom. Each section, therefore, has a theoretical component, a theory we seek to bring to life through everyday examples. After encouraging you to reflect on the way that you *think*, we offer ideas and guidance as to what you can next *do* in service of becoming a wiser, more effective leader. The five mantras are, in order:

1 Commit to reflective learning
2 Know yourselves
3 Transcend yourselves
4 Think meta
5 Do dialogue

1 Commit to reflective learning

Dilip Jeste and colleagues[21] asked 30 wisdom experts to rate characteristics of wisdom on a scale of one to nine. Self-reflection scored 8.6, the second highest ranking characteristic out of 47 measured. Few leaders would push back on the importance of learning. They recognize that learning is important, but they nevertheless fail to embrace just how important learning is or learn how to learn most effectively. Many leaders these days feel overwhelmed by the demands of their work. Learning is always on the list of things to do but rarely makes it to the top of the list. Or else learning is framed as a specific activity to engage in once or twice a year.

For the wise leader, learning is a way of being. The wise leader is open to experience, curious, and open to multiple perspectives. The wise leader is an explorer, continually seeking to probe, discover and understand. The wise leader doesn't only understand the importance of reflection but knows how to reflect, and actively engages in various forms of reflection. Our research tells us that more is not always better when it comes to reflecting. Important also are the *what* and the *how* of reflection. Wise leaders reflect to become more self-aware, learning lessons that guide future behaviour. Wise leaders spend more time exploring the deeper meaning of an event, adopting a non-defensive, self-critical, and open stance to learning. This process of reflective learning is deep and profound, yielding complex, growth-oriented lessons and insights.

2 Know yourselves

Wise people are more likely to question themselves and their intuitions[22]. To be wise means understanding the world and our place within it. We cannot stand aside from the world and pretend we have an objective perspective on the world. We are a part of the world, and the world is a part of us. To begin an exploration of ourselves in the world we start with an inspection of self. Most definitions of wisdom include self-awareness. How well do we know ourselves? To what extent do we understand our response to the world? To what extent do we understand the impact of our behaviours on the rest of the world?

Yet our existing efforts to facilitate greater self-awareness may be flawed. The leadership literature almost always depicts people as unitary entities defined by a single set of beliefs, motivations, and experiences. To become a great leader, so the story goes, a leader must develop a deep understanding of his/her 'true' self, then behave in accordance with that self at all times. Behaving in accordance with one's true self is often referred to as being authentic. We conduct personality tests and 360° feedback surveys, interpreting the findings as if they reflect the operation of a single self. Yet there is no evidence to support the idea that there is one me or one you. We all behave differently in different circumstances. We all have the same design of the brain, and there is no evidence that there exists a single centre of self in that brain. The only evidence for the existence of a single self is our subjective sense of being. This sense of self may be comforting, in that it gives us a sense of being in control, but it is likely illusory. There is more evidence to support the idea that we are not one, but many. Multiplicity theories have been around for a long time.

Authenticity, through this lens, is not about a single self in control of all its actions. It is about the extent to which we understand different aspects of our selves and the ways in which those different aspects are aware of each other and work together collaboratively. This way of exploring the self acknowledges the complexity of the self. The wise leader doesn't place herself in a two-by-two matrix or categorize herself as one of sixteen different types. The wise leader embraces her complexity and accepts that she will never become wholly self-aware. Self-awareness is a journey. The wise leader has a sophisticated understanding of her selves, is adaptable, and can bring the most effective version of her selves to the situation.

3 Transcend yourselves

To understand ourselves is one thing, to be able to simultaneously distance ourselves from our worldview is another thing. Our capacity to self-transcend determines the extent to which we can reflect on an issue from afar and disentangle ourselves from our dearly held beliefs, emotions, and certainties[23]. To self-transcend I must not only recognize who I am, but I how came to be, and how I continue to come to be. I need to have a sense of my different selves; where they came from, when they emerged, and how they continue to evolve. Many of our selves were formed early in life. The part of me that is self-critical, for example, my 'inner critic', may have been formed early in childhood, a consequence of continually being told I wasn't good enough. But not all my selves emerged in childhood. We can create new selves at any time to help us navigate life's challenges. I am not purely a manifestation of my genetics. My selves grow and evolve through my interactions with other people. The more aware I am of this co-creative process, the more purposeful I can be in my efforts to shape those selves and their relationships with each other.

The better I understand my selves and recognize the processes through which those selves are born and continue to evolve, the better able I am to stand aside from those selves and see them engage with each other and with other people. To become a wiser leader is about becoming more aware of my selves in relation to others. It is in this section that we connect ideas of multiple selves, and co-creation, with theories of adult development. Later stages of adult development depict a self-transcendent self, a self who thinks of his interactions with others in terms of collisions. These are collisions of different life experiences, different values, and different ways of looking at the world. Through this lens, I don't take these collisions personally. I see a collision as an opportunity to explore you and me. I am curious, not defensive. I am curious as to what it is about my way of approaching the world that triggers something in you and vice-versa. Again, this is no easy task. This way of approaching the world demands a different way of thinking.

Adult development theory describes different ways of thinking and suggests how people evolve from one way of thinking to another. Most contemporary adult development theories are linear and singular. We are one self at one position on a linear scale of development. These accounts don't resonate with us or the leaders with whom we work. Rather than think of adult development as progression up a scale it may be more useful to think of my different selves all being at different stages of development. I may feel utterly confident when one of my more developed selves is running the show, but less confident when a different self is running the show. And these selves operate at different levels in different contexts. Our work in the leader identity space has brought these ideas to life in many different cultural contexts. Leaders talk about the ways in which they consciously bring some parts of themselves as a leader to their work context and other parts of themselves to their lives at home and in their communities. The multiplicity perspective helps us recognize that we are all highly complex, we all have multiple identities, and we must continue to develop our understanding of our selves through this lens if we are to become more effective leaders. The wise leader is committed to this learning journey and has a sophisticated understanding of self that includes an understanding of how all her inner selves make meaning of the world. This helps the wise leader to take on challenges that other leaders find more daunting.

4 *Think* meta!

Much of the narrative so far has been inwardly focussed. This is the work we need to do if we are to succeed in thinking differently. Wise leaders also think differently about change. They recognize the limitations of their own thinking[24]. They acknowledge uncertainty[25] and are tolerant of ambiguity[26]. They are adept at solving unformulated, poorly defined problems with no obvious solutions[27]. They have different strategies for influencing and seeking to guide change. In the fourth section of the book, we consider how wise leaders think about change.

In these days of complexity and uncertainty, leaders find themselves asked to think 'systemically'. The inference is that they need to think somehow more astutely about the world around them. The problem is that few people take the time to define what thinking systemically means. There are at least five different broad ways of defining what it means to think systemically, each of which is quite different and which we detail in this book. The wise leader can think through all five of these lenses. Ultimately the wise leader thinks 'meta-systemically', recognizing the value of all the other ways of thinking *and* recognizing their limitations.

5 *Do* dialogue

Wise leaders engage in dialogue. They engage in dialogical thinking, enabling them to engage more effectively with others, curious as to what they are thinking - they can see problems from different perspectives[28]. They are empathetic and able to manage their emotions. This capacity to engage with others more effectively enables them to deal with complex challenges and to feel more confident tackling new experiences[29]. Once I have formed a view of the world around me and how it operates, I need to engage with it effectively if I am to be influential. I need to *do* stuff.

In Part Five we talk about the significance of dialogue. By 'dialogue' we don't mean 'conversation'. Dialogue is a particular type of conversation. When we engage in dialogue, we come prepared to listen without prejudice to what the other person is saying, suspending our convictions, opinions, and beliefs. And we come prepared to say what needs to be said – respectfully. It is easy to define dialogue, but much more difficult to put it into practice. Talking about dialogue is important because it opens our eyes to the essence of change and the importance of dialogue in influencing change.

The wise leader acknowledges complexity, recognizes she cannot control change, and understands that her role is to influence. The best way to influence is to create a space in which people can make sense of things for themselves. The wise leader understands how people are making sense of events because she is constantly listening to what people are saying. She is good at expressing what she is thinking and feeling, without being afraid that people may disagree, excited that some new, hitherto unthought-of, course of action may emerge.

These five mantras are our attempt to achieve a deeper understanding of wisdom, and to build a foundation upon which we can take practical steps in service of becoming wiser. In crafting this book, we have brought together two bodies of work. We have referred extensively to both the literature on wisdom and the wisdom on leadership development, particularly psychological perspectives on leadership. We have been delighted with the extent to which the two bodies of literature appear to complement each other. We have drawn also upon our own original research over the last 10–15 years, our extensive experiences as leaders, and our combined 40+ years' experience developing and coaching leaders across different countries and multiple industries. This is, we realize, just one attempt to explore further the notion of wise leadership. Nevertheless, we hope you find it insightful and useful.

References

1. Kunzmann, U. & Gluck, J. (2019). Wisdom and Emotion. In: R.J. Sternberg & J. Gluck [Eds.]. *The Cambridge Handbook of Wisdom.* Cambridge.
2. Flynn, J.R. (1987). Massive IQ Gain in 14 Nations: What IQ Tests Really Measure. *Psychological Bulletin, 101*(*2*), 171–191.
3. Winslow Taylor, F. (1911). *The Principles of Scientific Management.* Harper & Brothers.
4. https://www.theguardian.com/business/2012/jan/15/sir-robert-horton
5. https://www.ft.com/content/2a42aa08-a261-11db-a187-0000779e2340
6. Browne, J. (2011). *Beyond Business. An Inspirational Memoir from a Visionary Leader.* Orion Books.
7. Parsons, H.M. (1974). What happened at Hawthorne? *Science, 183*(*4128*), 922–932.
8. For example, https://eqi.org/eitests.htm
9. Yang, S.Y. (2011). Wisdom Displayed Through Leadership: Exploring Leadership-related Wisdom. *The Leadership Quarterly*, *22*(*4*), 616–632.
10. Edmondson, R. & Woerner, M.H. (2019). Sociocultural Foundations of Wisdom. In: R.J. Sternberg & J. Gluck [Eds.]. *The Cambridge Handbook of Wisdom.* Cambridge.
11. Bellah, R., Madsen, R., Sullivan, W., Swidler, A., & Tipton, S. (1996). *Habits of the Heart: Individualism and Commitment in American Life*, 2nd edition. University of California Press.

12. Humphreys, S. (1961). *The Wisdom of Buddhism*. Random House.
13. Sternberg, R.J. (1998). A Balance Theory of Wisdom. *Review of General Psychology, 2*, 347–365.
14. Baltes, P.B. & Staudinger, U.M. (2000). Wisdom: A Metaheuristic (Pragmatic) to Orchestrate Mind and Virtue Toward Excellence. *American Psychologist, 55*, 122–136.
15. Edmondson, R. & Woerner, M.H. (2019). Sociocultural Foundations of Wisdom. In: R.J. Sternberg & J. Gluck [Eds.]. *The Cambridge Handbook of Wisdom*. Cambridge.
16. Sternberg, R.J. (1985). Implicit Theories of Intelligence, Creativity, and Wisdom. *Journal of Personality and Social Psychology, 71*, 746–762.
17. Swartwood, J. & Tiberius, V. (2019). Philosophical Foundations of Wisdom. In: R.J. Sternberg & J. Gluck [Eds.]. *The Cambridge Handbook of Wisdom*. Cambridge.
18. Ardelt, M. (2008). Wisdom, Religiosity, Purpose in Life, and Death Attitudes of Aging Adults. In: A. Tomer, G.T. Eliason, P.P. Wong [Eds.]. *Existential and Spiritual Issues in Death Attitudes*. Lawrence Erlbaum Associates.
19. Sternberg, R. & Hagen, E.S. (2019). Teaching and Wisdom. In: R.J. Sternberg & J. Gluck [Eds.]. *The Cambridge Handbook of Wisdom*. Cambridge.
20. Sternberg, R. & Hagen, E.S. (2019). Teaching and Wisdom. In: R.J. Sternberg & J. Gluck [Eds.]. *The Cambridge Handbook of Wisdom*. Cambridge.
21. Jeste, D.V., Ardelt, M., Blazer, D., Kraemer, H.C., Vaillant, G., & Meeks, T.W. (2010). Expert Consensus on Characteristics of Wisdom: A Delphi Method Study. *The Gerontologist, 50*, 668–680.
22. Sternberg, R. & Gluck J. (2019). Wisdom, Morality, and Ethics. In: R.J. Sternberg & J. Gluck [Eds.]. *The Cambridge Handbook of Wisdom*. Cambridge.
23. Santos, H.C., Huynh, A.C., & Grossman, I. (2017). Wisdom in a Complex World: A Situated Account of Wise Reasoning and its Development. *Social and Personality Psychology Compass, 11(10)*.
24. Birren, J.E., & Svensson, C.M. (2005). Wisdom in History. In: R.J. Sternberg & J. Jordan [Eds.]. *The Handbook of Wisdom: Psychological Perspectives*. Cambridge University Press.
25. Oakes, H., Brienza, J.P., Elnakouri, A., & Grossman, I. (2019). Wise Reasoning. In: R.J. Sternberg & J. Gluck [Eds.]. *The Cambridge Handbook of Wisdom*. Cambridge.
26. Sternberg, R.J. (1998). A Balance Theory of Wisdom. *Review of General Psychology, 2*, 347–365.
27. Sternberg, R.J. (2019). Why People Often Prefer Wise Guys to Guys Who Are Wise. In: R.J. Sternberg & J. Gluck [Eds.]. *The Cambridge Handbook of Wisdom*. Cambridge.
28. Paul, R. (1985). Dialectical Reasoning: Developing Minds. In: A.L. Costa [Ed.]. *Developing Minds: A Resource Book for Teaching*. Association for Supervision and Curriculum Development.
29. Gluck, J. (2019). The Development of Wisdom During Adulthood. In: R.J. Sternberg & J. Gluck [Eds.]. *The Cambridge Handbook of Wisdom*. Cambridge.

Part One

Commit to Reflective Learning

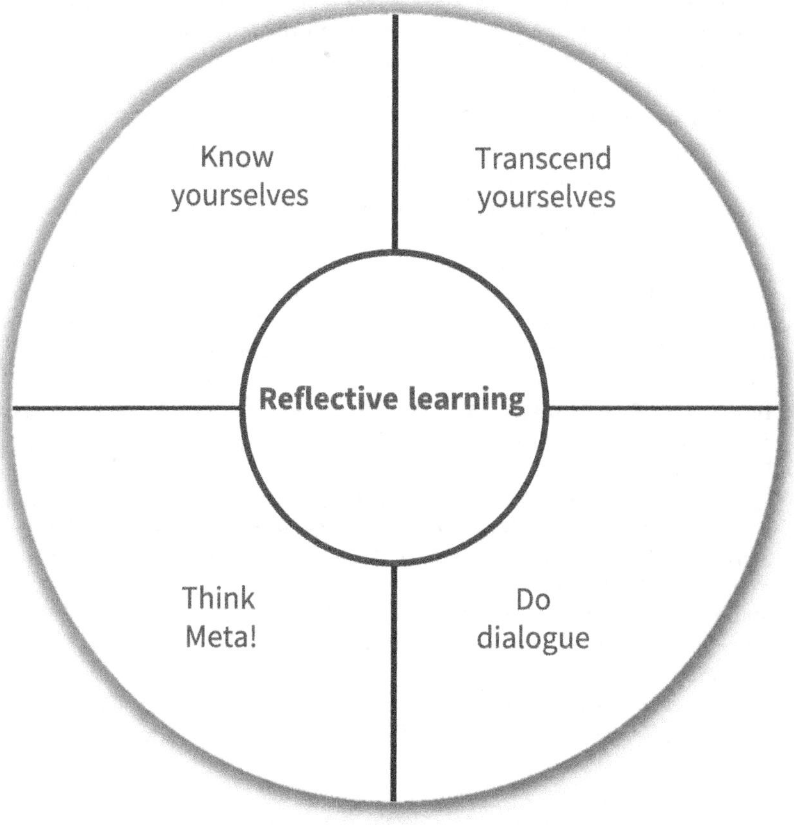

DOI: 10.4324/9781003284826-2

A leadership myth

Leaders Just Need to Reflect More Often

John was feeling stressed. He had two vacancies on his team which were proving difficult to fill but demands from the senior executive team continued unabated. He started work at eight in the morning and finished at eight at night, working later if need be. He felt tired all the time as did most of his team. He knew he needed to have a conversation with his manager to address the unsustainable workload, but he didn't have time to think about what to say – he was too busy getting stuff done. He felt like he was on a treadmill and Christmas seemed a long way off. He certainly wouldn't be getting any holidays before Christmas. Then Maria resigned, saying that while she liked him, liked the team, and liked the organization, she just couldn't keep working the hours she was working. A competitor offered her a similar role with a 15% increase in salary. She had spoken to members of her new team who all said they felt comfortable managing a good work-life balance.

John didn't know what to say. The prospect of continuing to work at the same pace without Maria felt impossible. He felt sick inside and realized he just had to make time to address some of the broader issues he and his team faced. After talking to a colleague, he determined to make time to stop and think about the bigger picture twice a week, at nine o'clock on a Monday morning and five o'clock on a Friday afternoon. He would consider what was going well, what wasn't going well, and what he needed to do to ensure the team was able to manage its workload better, whilst still achieving outcomes.

After his first reflection session, he resolved to get the team together for two hours to discuss how they could work together more efficiently, and to speak to his line manager about pushing back on requests from the executive team. He gathered the team on Wednesday, but the meeting didn't yield great outcomes. Two people were missing, pleading overwork. Those who came looked exhausted and spent most of the session explaining what wasn't working. Each time John tried to steer the conversation to a solution, people just sighed and resumed complaining. The meeting with his line manager didn't go well either. She seemed sympathetic but told him that everyone was having to work hard. Everyone was down on staff but if the business didn't deliver planned revenue targets, then the company would have to downsize even further.

On Friday John made time to sit and reflect on what had happened that week. He recalled how lost he felt working with the team, unable to get them to think about what they could improve. Two members of the team seemed determined that the only solution was for him, John, to talk to the senior executive team. He secretly wished they weren't on his team; talking to them just made him feel depressed, but he couldn't possibly do without them. It all seemed a bit hopeless. He reflected on the meeting with his line manager. He had made sure he prepared for the meeting. He spelled out clearly the tasks his team was working on and the resources they had available. He explained that he and others were working 12-hour days plus weekends. He explained that the team couldn't possibly continue to meet expectations with Maria gone, and explained his fears that more people would soon leave unless the workload was reduced, at least until he could find new staff. His line manager told him to persevere with recruitment and think about what else he could do to motivate his team. It wasn't just unfair; it was stupid. Soon he wouldn't have a team at all. He sat and mulled it all over for twenty minutes before going home. Next Monday he thought again about the two issues and resolved to have another crack at it, one day when he had time. The next Friday he made time to reflect again, but he just ended up more depressed.

John made time to reflect, but reflection didn't help. It is a myth that all we need to do to resolve all our issues is make time to sit and ponder those problems. We talk a lot about the need to make time to reflect, taking for granted that we know how best to reflect. The research suggests otherwise. If we want to develop as leaders, we must do more than make time to reflect. We need to consider *why* we reflect (the purpose of reflection) and *how* we reflect, and what we actually do during that reflection time.

Theory

The wisdom literature tells us that experience is important, indeed many definitions equate wisdom with life experience. But if becoming wiser was just about gaining life experience we would expect a strong correlation between age and wisdom which research suggests is not the case[1]. Lots of people have lots of experience, but they are not all wise. And some people don't have much experience at all, and yet do seem wise. As John Dewey said, '*We do not learn from experience. We learn from reflecting on experience*'[2].

We intuitively know that we need to reflect more often. However, the wisdom literature and our own research tell us we must also consider *how* we reflect. Nic Weststrate distinguishes between the why, how, and how often people reflect[3]. Reflecting more often, he suggests, may have little impact on wisdom. More important are the *why* and the *how*. The amount of time a person spends in self-reflection does not predict how wise that person is likely to be unless that reflection is of a certain quality and form[4]. Some people may spend significant time in self-reflection but be learning unwise lessons and insights from that process[5].

For Socrates wisdom was a critical process, the process of learning how to live an examined life[6]. The question then for leaders is, how much time do you spend examining yourself as a leader? How much effort do you assign to understanding yourself and your motivations and your behaviours? How much effort do you expend in examining yourself in relation to others? This process of self-examination, we believe, is part of the reflective process. We must not only get out there and interact with the world, but we must also make a conscious effort to learn from those experiences.

You will notice we have placed a commitment to reflective learning at the heart of the five mantras. There has been much debate in the wisdom world, should we regard self-reflection as an antecedent of wisdom, as an associated competency, or as a key mechanism driving the accrual of wisdom (Figure 1.1)? We align ourselves with those who see it as intrinsic to our quest to become wiser leaders.

To what extent are you a committed and reflective learner? In many organisations the learning function conduct learning needs analyses and then

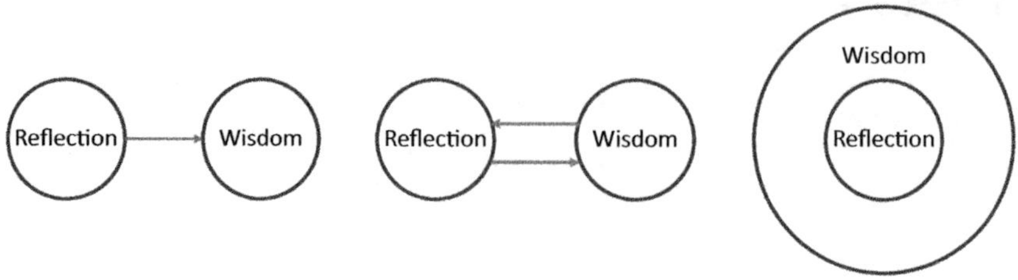

Figure 1.1 The role of reflection in becoming wiser.

tell people what they need to learn. If, in your role as a leader, attending these kinds of programs is what constitutes your learning strategy, then we question the extent you are committed to learning. Those programs may be useful and interesting and may provoke some learning, but the commitment to learning we're talking about comes from within. We're talking about your personal commitment to reflective learning, to ongoing deep reflection on your experiences as they occur, not your commitment to comply with someone else's view as to what you should be learning.

If we are to become wiser then we need to commit to learning and we need to understand more about the learning process, and how to learn. In the rest of this section, we explore how to get better at learning. Here we mean learning as a continual process rather than a set of events or series of learning modules. Here we're talking about an ongoing process of learning from everyday events, of *reflective* learning. Our research suggests that wise people habitually reflect on events and that they reflect in order to learn more about themselves, and the world around them. The second finding we discuss is that wise leaders reflect upon the growth of all, not just the growth of self. Wise reflection is self-reflection, but it is not selfish reflection. Finally, we consider the finding that wise reflection includes a focus on the past, present, and future. Wise reflection is not just reminiscence or rumination, it is an active process of integration of past, present, and future perspectives in service of greater learning.

1 *Self*-reflection involves reflecting on the self

A key aspect of wisdom is openness to learning[7], being open to having our basic beliefs about life challenged[8]. Notice that when he did make time to reflect, John's focus was purely external. He spent his time thinking about the challenges he was facing, but his focus was squarely on the behaviour of others. This is reflection, but it isn't self-reflection, and it doesn't speak to a willingness to consider his own role in what was happening. Ask yourself – when you reflect (if you reflect), why do you reflect? There are lots of possible reasons for reflecting. For example:

- Because someone told me it was a good idea
- Because I'm feeling overwhelmed and need to prioritize my tasks
- Because the team isn't working well together, and we need to get clear who is doing well and who might need to be moved on
- Because I have a presentation to do next week and haven't thought carefully enough about what I want to say

All are useful, but none of these reflections will help us to become wiser. Nic Weststrate's research and our research suggest that wise people reflect primarily to deepen their understanding of self. This is different from reflecting in order to absolve oneself of blame or guilt, or to identify a few quick steps to move forward, or to work out what someone else needs to do differently. We often encounter leaders, usually insecure and not very wise leaders, who spend much of their reflection time working out how to make themselves look good in service of getting promoted. These leaders don't always reflect on self. To reflect on self feels scary – who knows what inconvenient truth might become apparent?

Nic Weststrate considers various aspects of reflection, including:

- Narrative coherence – coming up with a good story that accounts for what happened
- Positive reframing – reframing a negative event into a positive event, providing resolution and closure
- Self-exploration – a non-defensive, self-critical analysis as to what I might have done differently

Narrative coherence is useful and correlates with enhanced levels of well-being. Coming up with a story that helps make sense of everything that happened makes me feel better, but it doesn't correlate with enhanced levels of wisdom. Positive reframing is also useful and correlates with our ability to adjust and adapt to events in the workplace. In other words, finding the positive aspects of an apparently negative event helps me resolve an issue in my own mind and move on. But it doesn't directly correlate with enhanced levels of wisdom. Self-exploration – spending time reflecting on me and the role I played in whatever just happened, *does* correlate with enhanced levels of wisdom. Judith Gluck and Susan Bluck's MORE Life Experience model of wisdom[9] features reflectivity, defined as one's motivation and ability to reflect deeply, complexly, and non-defensively on one's own life experiences and the experiences of others. Wise people are curious, needing to understand what is happening amidst complexity and needing to understand themselves in relation to that complexity.

Finding out more about ourselves is like finding out more about a character in a book. The author of a good book doesn't tell us about her characters – she shows us. She doesn't write 'George was brave and fearless', instead she presents George with a challenge that he rises to and overcomes. We form perspectives on the characters in a book by accompanying them on their journeys and noticing what they do when faced with adversity. The author expedites the process by presenting characters with challenge after challenge, leaving us to make our own sense of their reactions. We learn about ourselves in the same way. I may tell myself I am an empathetic individual, but one day I find myself berating a colleague for the quality of their work. I surprise myself with just how annoyed I become. I'm alarmed when I reflect on how I responded. What do I do now? Do I try and forget about it and think about something more pleasant? Do I blame the individual for doing such a terrible job? Do I quickly forgive myself for being over-tired? Or do I make time to confront what happened, explore it further, and seek to understand better what happened? We learn more about ourselves by reflecting on our responses to unexpected events.

In navigating complexity, we are likely to experience multiple unexpected events. To act wisely in a complex situation requires the ability to step back and think clearly about the situation and to reflect upon what we are thinking and feeling at that moment[10]. Some people retreat in the face of challenge, seeking to push away uncertainty and identify a nice simple solution. The wise leader embraces ambiguity and the opportunity to learn from attempting to navigate that ambiguity. Wisdom is founded on a deep desire to know, including a desire to know more about ourselves. Wise people look beyond the simple surface of complex problems. They explore deeper meanings. Wise people have a profound motivation to learn and are open to new ways of thinking, feeling, and doing. They recognize their limitations and are humble.

In our own research, we found that leaders with relatively high levels of self-efficacy were more likely to *self*-reflect, were more likely to be self-aware, and were more aware of their internal thoughts and emotions[11]. Looking back now at John's reflections, we see little curiosity as to how he might have been contributing to his dilemma, and no evidence that he was reflecting in the moment. If his team were overworked and stressed, if his line manager was unhelpful and unsympathetic, if no one was out there looking for new team members, what role was John playing in all of that? To what extent was he contributing to the situation? To what extent was his problem co-created? To what extent did his reluctance to think about what was happening at the moment exacerbate his difficulties? What got in the way of him having more robust conversations with the leaders of his organization? What did John have to learn about *himself* in reflecting on this experience?

2 Reflecting in service of others vs reflecting in service of self

In our research, we found that leaders high in self-efficacy engage in a reflective learning process that we called *reflective positivity*, while leaders with low levels of self-efficacy do not. Leaders low in self-efficacy may have aspired to reflect more often, but they didn't reflect in the same way. Reflective positivity includes reflection on self, and also a propensity to reflect with others and about others, a process we call *symbiotic positivity*[12]. The process is *positive* in that these leaders were actively choosing, in the moment, to receive feedback in a way that was about cultivating possibility. They reflected on challenging feedback through a positive lens, based on a strong belief in their own potential and the potential of others. They consciously prioritized positivity, seeking out future possibilities even in the most challenging of circumstances. The process is *symbiotic* in that it represents a commitment to learning with-and-through-others[13]. For example, one participant in the research study said, '*As I'm reflecting, I tend not to separate too much between my success versus the team success*'. These leaders actively chose an abundance mentality based on a belief that there is room for everyone to succeed. Their reflections on self were grounded in a broader context of wanting *everyone* to succeed and grow together. These leaders tended not to think in terms of hierarchy, instead, they actively reflected on ways in which they could grow symbiotically with the people around them, often in real time. Our research showed that leaders lower in self-efficacy aspired to symbiotic positivity, but their reflections were more likely to be focussed on their own learnings and not the development of their team. This is a more hierarchical and individualistic perspective on leadership that limits the possibilities for leadership and problem-solving.

The wisdom literature supports our findings. To become wiser, I must seek out new experiences. I must be prepared to step outside my comfort zone. I must see new challenges not only in terms of the possibility of failure but also as opportunities to extend myself and learn. But stepping outside my comfort zone isn't a matter of stepping out into the unknown and winging it. Taking on a new challenge is about carefully weighing up where I feel equipped to succeed and where I don't. Being confident that I am committing to climbing a steep hill, not to jumping off a cliff.

The wisdom literature tells us that becoming wiser is a joint endeavour[14]. I need to put aside the idea that I am expected to navigate this new challenge by myself and instead engage others to help me succeed. That might be a few technical experts, people who have an expertise that I don't. That might be a few people who've taken on similar challenges in the past or who just seem to me to be good at learning. Many western societies are highly individualistic. Accordingly, in many organizations, development is seen to be the responsibility of the individual. Contrast that to *ubuntu*, a commitment to universal sharing that connects all human beings. Or the Chinese proverbs, '*in a group of three people, there will always be one person I can learn from*,' and '*when you teach someone, both teacher and student benefit*.' The wisdom literature encourages us to question our motivation for learning. Many writers frame the purpose of learning to be the acquisition of a deeper understanding of life in service of improving the quality of one's own life *and the lives of others*[15].

Notice that John spent his reflection time reflecting by himself about his problem. His thinking is quite individualistic. And instead of looking for possibility in the challenges he is facing, he appears locked into a deficit mindset. Yes, he says he is concerned about the well-being of his staff, but he doesn't seem very interested in understanding the issue through their eyes, indeed he wishes some of his staff weren't on his team because he finds talking to them makes him depressed. He isn't thinking about what his staff members might best do for themselves, or how they might all grow together in dealing with the challenges they face. Indeed, he wishes Maria were still on the team because she made his life easier. Yes, he got the team together to think about how to work more efficiently but he didn't open up the conversation to think more broadly about the issue or frame it as a possible learning opportunity. He didn't want to hear the team talk about what was difficult and he felt burdened that two of his team members were looking to him to address the issue with the executive team, instead of feeling grateful that they opened up to him.

We talk a lot about reflection as an individual endeavour, however, our research shows that reflection is best regarded as a collective endeavour. Research suggests that people who talk to others and make time to reflect on those conversations respond with greater wisdom than those who do not. Our research suggests also that wisdom is cultivated through reflecting in the moment, in the face of our hardest challenges. Choosing to see possibility, and committing to growing with and through others, moves us away from narrow, individualistic interpretations of our world to a more collective and collaborative perspective.

Intriguing, and relevant to Part Two, is the discovery that people who just *imagine* talking to others also show higher levels of wisdom.

3 Thinking past and present in service of future

In our research, we found that people scoring high in leader self-efficacy moved fluidly in their reflections between different time frames[16]. For example, one person said: '*I'm always thinking about where we're going, not where we are, to some degree. I'm always thinking about multiple perspectives and contexts that I'm adjusting to*'. Leaders who scored lower in self-efficacy were less likely to move fluidly between past and recent-past experience and future intentions and were more likely to focus only on present experience. For example, '*You can't dwell on the past when you're focused on the present*'.

Nic Weststrate distinguishes between self-reflection and reminiscence[17], a present/past-focused process of recollection that doesn't necessarily involve any processing or analysis. He cites evidence that wiser people use self-reflection to learn lessons from the past that guide future behavior. Reminiscence by itself doesn't lead to learning. Through our research and practical experience, we have learned that these differences in how we choose to orient to time have a significant impact on the resources that are available to us. If we are focused only on the present, with no reflective attention given to relevant past experiences or future intentions, we limit our thinking. By choosing to broaden our time horizons, actively inquiring into how we may have dealt with this challenge in the past, or recombining our experiences to carve out new pathways, we open up new possibilities.

When we consider John's reflections through the lens of time, we can see that they are focused mostly on his current predicament. He is focused on why life is so hard right now. It seems like he has constructed a story to explain what is happening, a story in which his staff are tired, depressed, and depressing, and in which his line manager is disinterested and stupid (a good example of *narrative coherence*). We don't hear much consideration about the past, a past in which his team members were more motivated and engaged, a past in which the organization willingly provided his team with adequate resources, a past in which others may have faced the same predicament as him and succeeded in leading the team forwards successfully. Nor do we hear much about what John might do next. His over-emphasis on the present makes the present feel overwhelming.

Wise reflection

In summary, then, wise leaders are committed to reflective learning. They make time to reflect and seek to learn from other leaders they perceive to be wise. They consciously choose to reflect in the midst of doing, progressively strengthening their capacity for reflecting in the moment. The wise leader reflects because she wants to understand more about herself and how she interacts with others. She is committed to becoming more self-aware. She seeks feedback on a regular basis and is self-critical and non-defensive, willing to direct her reflections inward, taking responsibility for her responses in service of becoming a better leader. The wise leader is actively committed not only to her own growth and development but to that of her team and function, and to the development of the organization as a whole. This is reflected in how she talks about reflection. There is less about me and I, and more about we and us, more about what we can learn and what might be possible for us all. And the wise leader thinks broadly. She thinks about the past to the extent it helps her to think about the future, and she thinks about the present, again in service of her own development.

How can you tell if a leader is committed to reflective learning? You can ask them questions like:

- How much time do you dedicate to learning?
- What are you learning about?
- What are you learning about yourself?
- What are you good at, and what might you get better at?

- How do you and your team reflect on how things are going?
- How open are you to learning from every exchange you have with people day to day?

Some leaders struggle to answer any of these questions. They work long hours, are tired, and are overwhelmed. They don't have a clear learning agenda. They don't spend time thinking about what they're good at and what they're not so good at unless prompted to do so by mandatory performance review processes. They don't seek out new information because when they do, occasionally, find time to step aside from work, they are too exhausted to do anything other than watch television. These leaders would agree that learning is important *and* would say that they're just too busy for learning ever to make it to the top of their list of priorities. They certainly don't see learning as an ongoing, in-the-moment, reflective process.

As we have seen in our practice and research, other leaders are more disciplined in their commitment to learning. They understand the value of experience and understand that with no actual commitment to learning, and no time spent reflecting, they will likely never truly benefit from the opportunities offered to them by their experiences. They hold strong intentions around two or three areas where they'd like to improve as leaders. They make time to reflect, and they reflect in the moment, in the process of leading. They see reflection as a team sport, not a solo activity performed only when alone.

This section is first in the book because you may find it useful to reflect upon your commitment to reflective learning in preparation before reading the rest of the book. Part Two is called *know yourselves*. In it, we will outline some principles for thinking about self. We hope you enjoy it, reflect on it, and that you learn something new.

Epilogue

John Reflects Differently

John's team was still understaffed. He was still working 70 hours a week. His staff were still deeply unhappy.

On Monday John left his phone at home and went for a walk in the park. He realized that nothing was going to change unless something fundamentally changed within himself. He noticed that he wasn't the only one struggling to meet the demands of the organization. He noted also that some people seemed to be doing OK. What was different about those teams? What would he need to do differently to lead his team forward more effectively? He could just walk away, and find an easier job working fewer hours, as Maria had done. But what then? What happened next time his team became overworked? Many of his friends worked in organizations just as busy as his.

He found himself feeling angry again about the behaviour of Luisa, his line manager. Every time he went to see her, she nodded sympathetically before telling him he just needed to suck it up. She didn't use those words exactly, but she might as well have done. She was working hard too, he knew. At least she made the time to talk to him. Some managers were impossible to reach. When she told him he needed to suck it up, he was listening to her personal mantra. That's what she told herself, and that's what she told him. He was going to have to manage conversations with her differently.

As he contemplated being more assertive, more forthright, he felt his stomach churn. He didn't like any form of confrontation. What would he do if Luisa got annoyed? He needed her to be OK. He needed to be able to call on her and needed her to approve of the work he was doing. He took a couple of deep breaths and reflected on past experiences when he had handled this kind of conversation well. There was no point in picking an argument. He would need to express himself differently. In reflecting on his more recent experiences, he recognized that he needed to find an entirely different way to engage.

He would go and see her again, he decided. He would restate his concerns around workload. Though he felt like delivering her an ultimatum, he wouldn't do that. He wasn't going to resign either, recognizing the significance of his current role in his desired future career path. There was nothing to be learned or gained by walking away – it would just leave her with a problem that would leave her working ever longer hours. She looked tired. He would restate his problems, then he would ask a lot of questions, a strategy he had deployed before but somehow recently forgotten. He would seek to understand what the world looked like through her eyes. Find out more about the organization and how it operated, some of the challenges she was facing. And find out more about her, her values, and way of thinking about the world. He needed to understand more before he could work out what best to do next and how they might grow through this together. As John walked home and reflected on his new intentions, he felt more energized, confident, and hopeful.

John didn't wait until Friday to reflect again upon his situation. He went to talk to Luisa and succeeded in staying calm and curious. He restated his concerns around workload and listened again as she explained that the whole organization was under-resourced. He didn't push back, not yet. He just asked questions and listened. As he waited outside the café on the street corner for his coffee, he recapped on what he had heard. He learned that:

- The recruitment team itself was understaffed. There was a long backlog of work and new recruitment was being strictly triaged. It wasn't at all clear how far up the queue his own needs were placed. Luisa was vague in her responses and became somewhat irritated when he persevered with his questioning. She visibly relaxed when he offered to speak directly to the hiring manager.
- The CEO recognized that people were under stress but didn't allow a lot of time for the senior executive team to discuss. His primary focus was delivering planned revenue numbers. The organization was 5% off target and he was pushing for everyone to make up the gap.
- Whilst John's team was just about hitting their numbers, Luisa's division was 9% down on plan and Luisa felt under pressure. She was working long hours working with three of John's counterparts trying to push performance.

As John reflected on the conversation, he recognized a few things about himself, namely:

- This was the first time in a long time he had asked Luisa so many questions. He had been assuming that she was on top of things, that she was in control. He recognized that he placed too much emphasis on hierarchy and not enough on relating to senior authority figures as human beings.
- He had spent no time at all reflecting on his peers and how they were going. They all looked stressed, but he hadn't spent much time thinking about what was going on for them – he was too focused on his own predicament.
- He didn't even know the hiring manager. He spoke often to some of the people reporting to the hiring manager but had no personal relationship himself.

He needed to reflect more broadly, network more widely, and adopt a much more curious mindset. He resolved to:

- Meet up with the hiring manager and learn more about what was happening in that part of the business, their challenges, their priorities, and how his own needs fit into the big picture.
- Meet up with all his peers to see how he could help. He was the longest serving member of the team and had more technical expertise than any of them. There might also be opportunities to identify and leverage some synergies if they thought a little differently about how to use their collective resources.
- Frame up some thoughts on the way forward, after those discussions, and present those to Luisa. His team was hitting their numbers and he didn't see why the whole division couldn't hit their numbers too if they went about things a bit differently.

John took five minutes to explain his thinking to his team the next time they met. He didn't expect the team to get too excited just yet, but he wanted to plant the seed. If they could see how useful they could be in helping the rest of the division to achieve better results, then they might see how much more they could contribute to the organization as a whole. This might help them feel more engaged, more pivotal to the success of the company. He recognized the need to create an environment more conducive to them all learning together. He would need to recruit a couple of new people quickly, not least to give the team confidence that the organization cared about them and their workloads. He had a couple of ideas in that space. First, he'd make a good case to the hiring manager to ensure his team's needs were appropriately taken care of. And he would put more effort into leveraging his own networks to find new people.

Things started to change for John. Not everything proceeded as planned, nor as quickly as planned, but things started to change and people become more hopeful. And John continued to learn things about himself he hadn't acknowledged before.

Self-development

Here are twenty questions you as a leader may find useful in seeking to become a more effective, wiser, learner. We suggest you pick a few questions in the first place, those that best resonate for you, and consider your response in some depth, over a period of time. As you experience yourself becoming a more committed and accomplished reflective learner, then you may come back and pick a few more. We don't see there being a great value in ticking off all 20 questions in one go. Think of the questions as thought provokers. Which two or three questions for you are most provocative?

Being intentional

In this section, we suggested that wise leaders are committed to their own learning. That likely means they have specific learning intentions, written down or otherwise. We don't mean a plan that someone else asked you to come up with, as part of an annual review process, or part of a learning program. We mean something you put together because you wanted to put it together – something you are committed to.

1 Do you have clear learning intentions?
2 If not, when will you get some?

Stepping outside your comfort zone

At the beginning of Part One, we talked about the importance of gaining new experience and making time to learn from that experience. Staying in the same role for a long period of time may feel comfortable and it may be tempting to stay in that role. Other times new challenges may be thrust upon us, and we may feel obliged to accept them without thinking through the possible value of that new experience. We wrote about being purposeful in taking on new challenges, and we talked about having a robust learning strategy which includes asking others for support. These questions are around the extent to which you are strategic about taking on new challenges.

3 How willing are you to step outside your comfort zone?
4 What will be your purpose in seeking out your next new challenging experience?
5 Who will you enroll in helping you learn from those experiences?

Making time to self-reflect

We point out in this section that just making time to reflect isn't enough. We want you to think also about how you reflect, and the extent to which you reflect in the moment. We suggest that reflection before, during, and after any experience is an essential component of any learning strategy. We suggested that wise leaders are purposeful in their reflection and spend some of their reflection time seeking to understand themselves better.

6 How often do you reflect and is that sufficient?
7 To what extent do you reflect in the moment? How could you strengthen this practice?
8 How often do you ask for feedback, seeking to understand how you are perceived by others?
9 How much of your reflection time is spent reflecting on you vs. the behaviour of others and factors in the external environment?
10 How much time will you spend on self-reflection over the next week/month?

Symbiotic positivity

We cited evidence that leaders with high levels of self-efficacy consciously choose to think positively, and choose to reflect on everyone's development, not just their own development.

11 When you are facing challenging situations, what do you reflect on? How can you shift your focus from what is wrong in the situation to what might be possible?
12 When in dialogue with people, how can you bring forth more gratitude and joy in your reflections with them?
13 To whose learning, other than your own, are you committed?
14 What, specifically, will you do over the next week/month/quarter in service of others' learnings?

We also suggest that wise leaders spend time reflecting with others. They don't spend all their time reflecting alone.

15 How could you and your team reflect together more effectively?
16 How much time do you spend with others, reflecting together?

Past, present, and future

We suggested that wise leaders integrate their reflections on the past, present, and future.

17 How much time do you spend reminiscing about the past, versus purposefully seeking to learn from the past?
18 How often do you make time to reflect in the moment, drawing on past successes and future goals, particularly when faced with a difficult or complex problem?

Reading this book

How will your approach to reflective learning show up in the way you read this book?

19 How will you capture useful insights?
20 When will you make the time to translate those insights into clear actionable commitments?

Designing interventions

As someone responsible for designing leadership development programs, we wonder what insights you have taken away from this section. We do a lot of program design ourselves and offer you the following thoughts.

1 Invite – don't coerce

Ralph Stacey has some interesting things to say about leadership development[18]. He suggests that leadership development programs are usually commissioned by HR professionals who work with consultancies to design programs. Often, none of the people designing a program have personal experience in leadership. Leadership programs are often designed with the needs of whole layers of management in mind, and everyone at that level of management is expected to attend. Programs are designed with reference to a standard set of leadership competencies on the basis that acquiring those competencies is all that is required to be a good leader.

Stacey is critical of this approach on at least two grounds. First, he suggests, the leadership literature doesn't accurately depict the life of real leaders. Real leaders spend a lot of time performing quite mundane tasks. Their lives are not extraordinary – they don't spend all their time visioning and strategizing, for example. They spend a lot of their time doing the work. The leadership literature talks about leaders as if they have lots of autonomy, whereas most leaders work within quite tight parameters in terms of what they can and cannot do. Program designers, therefore, need to be careful that they design something relevant, appropriate, and practical, and avoid creating offerings based on idealized notions of leadership.

Second, program designs emphasizing generic competencies, presenting simple models that enable participants to enact those competencies, don't reflect the complexities of modern leadership. This approach assumes we can break down leadership into relatively simple tasks and implies that the program designers know best. If leaders are subsequently measured as to the extent they are displaying these generic competencies, then the approach may be coercive. No room is left for leaders to work out for themselves how to respond to the complexities they face, and no discretion is available for them to make their own choices.

Stacey describes leadership in terms of practical judgment. Practical judgment is a similar idea to practical wisdom. It is the idea that we develop as leaders over time, through experience and our reflections on that experience. Stacey defines practical judgment as '*the experience-based ability to notice more of what is going on and intuit what is most important about a situation*'[19]. Stacey suggests that coaching and mentoring have important roles to play in fostering practical wisdom and that the greatest contribution a coach can make is encourage the development of self-awareness.

All of this suggests we should avoid trying to push leaders toward becoming externally defined versions of an ideal leaders. Such an approach leaves little room for leaders to develop their own personal sense of what it means to be a good leader, or their own leadership identity. That doesn't mean leadership development programs cannot be useful. But it does require a paradigm shift on our part. We need to hold lightly our depiction of great leadership and resist the temptation to build definitive leadership competency frameworks. Instead, we can usefully *offer* curious leaders new theories and ideas and create the space for them to experiment with those ideas – if they so choose. There is no point in forcing leaders to attend leadership programs. Participants must be curious and interested, committed to reflective learning. If they are not committed to learn, they may show up, they make take notes, they may enjoy your program and give it a 10/10 rating, but they are unlikely to embark on the work required to change the way they behave back in the workplace.

Our first principle then, in designing any leadership program, is to *invite* leaders to attend if they want to and ensure that there is no penalty attached to declining the invitation. Indeed, we would like to have leaders banging down the door to attend a program. The more energized our participants, the more committed to learn, the greater the outcomes are likely to be for everyone.

2 Make time for reflection

A few years ago, we were invited to coach people going through a leadership program. As part of the exercise, we were invited to attend the program itself. The program ran from nine in the morning to seven at night. The program was packed with models and theories. When we asked the facilitator why the program had been designed that way, he said that leaders these days were expected to work long hours, and to be productive during those hours, and so they should be able to manage an intense learning experience. We watched a classroom of bright, eager learners slowly wilt and droop. By the end of each day, people lay slumped across tables. Little time was provided for genuine reflection, and little was learned. That is an extreme example, but we frequently see reflection time gradually squeezed down as program designs are finalized, sacrificed for 'essential content'. If you want your leaders to become wiser you need to create space for them to reflect, alone and with each other. You need to help them understand that reflecting-while-doing is a muscle that they can strengthen.

3 Teach people how to reflect

As we explain in this section, we talk a lot about the importance of reflection, not so much about *how* to reflect. Our suggestion is that you dedicate time to help your leaders become more proficient at reflection. Share with them what the literature and research, particularly our research on reflective positivity, have to say about effective reflection, and take them through the key elements of reflective positivity as outlined in this section. For example, the importance of *self*-reflection, symbiotic positivity, and connecting past lessons, with present experience, and future intention.

4 Group coaching

Wisdom is not a private matter. People make sense of the world around them together. They define together what wisdom means in their community, and how to attain wisdom. Monks in a Tibetan monastery said that while they felt everyone has the capacity to be wise, everyone needs assistance from others[20]. Teaching is a form of support, but teachers often teach from an elevated position, they play the role of experts. How do you qualify to be an expert in practical wisdom? Teaching is an appropriate means through which to teach technical knowledge, but a focus on technical knowledge is believed by many to be a *barrier* to attaining wisdom[21]. A better approach is to create forums in which people can learn from each other and support each other in their learnings.

Teaching people how to reflect through lectures and slides may enable people to grasp the principles of effective reflection intellectually, but that by itself is unlikely to have a great impact. Better, we find, to provide people with the reflective experience. You might already provide people with individual coaching on your leadership programs. Individual coaching is often well-received, but sometimes the experience can be ho-hum for both coach and coachee. Much more effective, we find, and consistent with the idea of symbiotic positivity, is to create the space for group coaching.

People are always surprised by just how impactful well-designed group coaching can be. We do a lot of group coaching. Group coaching is a great process around which to build development programs. We recommend working with small groups for 90 to 120 minutes every few weeks. The role of the group coach is to help the group agree ground rules, rules that enable people to feel safe sharing their experiences with others. The group coach provides a structure for a session, again enabling group members to feel comfortable, knowing that someone will make sure the group stays on track. The group coach enables everyone to speak and to be heard and encourages people to 'coach' each other. By coaching each other we mean that group members ask each other questions, to help each other co-reflect. Group members often come to a session energized to offer advice and give solutions. Sometimes this is helpful and often it isn't. Group members who come to a session hoping that others will help them think things through can feel embarrassed or diminished when others assume they know the answer. We ask group members only to offer advice and suggestion when explicitly asked to do so. It is the role of the group coach to help people work together effectively, and to role model great listening and curiosity.

People often come to group coaching unsure of what to expect. We send them short pre-reads sharing our research into what makes an effective group. Most people find group coaching insightful and supportive. It is often a huge relief to leaders to discover that they are not alone in facing some of the challenges they are experiencing. They are hungry to learn from colleagues facing the same issues, colleagues in the same boat as they are. People usually find the experience and wisdom of their colleagues more helpful and inspirational than anything an external facilitator or consultant has to offer. If you haven't tried group coaching, we strongly recommend you integrate group coaching into your leadership and development programs. You might also apply group coaching to your cultural change agendas, providing leaders at every level with the opportunity to reflect and learn with-and-through each other, as an effective way to evolve the cultural narrative.

5 Run your programs over a l-o-n-g period of time

It's tempting to condense a leadership program into two or three days, or a week. When bringing people in from different locations this often feels like the only practical approach. The problem with this approach when seeking to cultivate wisdom in leaders, is that leaders learn through reflecting on their experiences. You can, of course, make your programs experiential. Set people tasks and create time for them to reflect on their achievement of those tasks. The problem with this approach is that little is at stake. To take someone outside their comfort zone requires that they take on a complex challenge, the solving of which is important to them. Your leaders are already busy. They already have plenty of challenges they are facing. These are their priorities. You don't need to create new challenges for them. Instead, structure your programs around the work. By all means, present new theories and ideas, but above all create time for your leaders to reflect on their work and to learn through reflection with each other.

Your 3Ps revisited

In the introduction to this book, we introduced you to the 3Ps: Philosophy, Purpose, and Practice. Your 3Ps are interconnected. The way you think about leadership (Philosophy) shapes both your Purpose and the way you behave (Practice) (Figure 1.2).

In this section, we have shared some theories and offered you some suggestions as to what you might do differently as a leader. Remember though, we said that we don't claim to have all the answers. We don't offer you a definitive version of wise leadership because our definitions of wisdom depend on the work that we do and the people with whom we interact. It is not our quest to tell you how to become a wise leader. Rather we seek to help you work out for yourself – who is the wise leader you aspire to be? The 3Ps is a simple framework that breaks that question down into sub-components. Based on what you have read so far then:

- What new ideas stood out for you? (philosophy)
- How now would you articulate your purpose in leading? (purpose)
- How might you now choose to behave differently as a leader? (practice)

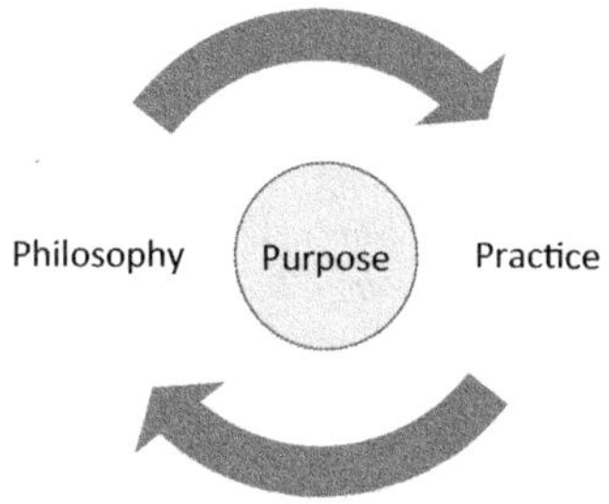

Figure 1.2 The 3Ps.

Similarly, as a leadership development professional:

- What new ideas stood out for you?
- How now would you articulate your purpose in designing and implementing leadership development programs?
- Has anything changed in terms of what your leadership programs are now likely to look like?

References

1. Gluck, J. (2019). The Development of Wisdom during Adulthood. In: R.J. Sternberg & J. Gluck [Eds.]. *The Cambridge Handbook of Wisdom*. Cambridge.
2. A famous quote, hard to find the original source. His best-known book is Experience and Nature, written in 1925.
3. Weststrate, N.M. (2019). The Mirror of Wisdom: Self-Reflection as a Developmental Precursor and Core Competency of Wise People. In: R.J. Sternberg & J. Gluck [Eds.]. *The Cambridge Handbook of Wisdom*. Cambridge.
4. Weststrate, N.M. (2019). The Mirror of Wisdom: Self-Reflection as a Developmental Precursor and Core Competency of Wise People. In: R.J. Sternberg & J. Gluck [Eds.]. *The Cambridge Handbook of Wisdom*. Cambridge.
5. Weststrate, N.M. (2019). The Mirror of Wisdom: Self-Reflection as a Developmental Precursor and Core Competency of Wise People. In: R.J. Sternberg & J. Gluck [Eds.]. *The Cambridge Handbook of Wisdom*. Cambridge.
6. Edmondson, R. & Woerner, M.H. (2019). Sociocultural Foundations of Wisdom. In: R.J. Sternberg & J. Gluck [Eds.]. *The Cambridge Handbook of Wisdom*. Cambridge.
7. Gluck, J. (2019). The Development of Wisdom during Adulthood. In: R.J. Sternberg & J. Gluck [Eds.]. *The Cambridge Handbook of Wisdom*. Cambridge.
8. Weststrate, N.M. (2019). The Mirror of Wisdom: Self-Reflection as a Developmental Precursor and Core Competency of Wise People. In: R.J. Sternberg & J. Gluck [Eds.]. *The Cambridge Handbook of Wisdom*. Cambridge.
9. Gluck, J., & Bluck, S. (2013). The MORE Life Experience Model: A Theory of the Development of Personal Wisdom. In: M. Ferrari & N. Weststrate [Eds.]. *The Scientific Study of Personal Wisdom*. Dordrecht.
10. Gluck, J. (2019). The Development of Wisdom during Adulthood. In: R.J. Sternberg & J. Gluck [Eds.]. *The Cambridge Handbook of Wisdom*. Cambridge.
11. Skinner, S. (2021). *Understanding the Influences on Leader Self-Efficacy: A Constructivist Grounded Theory Study*. Doctorate thesis. University of Wollongong.
12. Skinner, S. (2021). *Understanding the Influences on Leader Self-Efficacy: A Constructivist Grounded Theory Study*. Doctorate thesis. University of Wollongong.
13. Skinner, S. (2021). *Understanding the Influences on Leader Self-Efficacy: A Constructivist Grounded Theory Study*. Doctorate thesis. University of Wollongong.
14. Edmondson, R. & Woerner, M.H. (2019). Sociocultural Foundations of Wisdom. In: R.J. Sternberg & J. Gluck [Eds.]. *The Cambridge Handbook of Wisdom*. Cambridge.
15. Gluck, J. (2019). The Development of Wisdom during Adulthood. In: R.J. Sternberg & J. Gluck [Eds.]. *The Cambridge Handbook of Wisdom*. Cambridge.

16. Skinner, S. (2021). *Understanding the Influences on Leader Self-Efficacy: A Constructivist Grounded Theory Study*. Doctorate thesis. University of Wollongong.
17. Weststrate, N.M. (2019). *The Mirror of Wisdom: Self-Reflection as a Developmental Precursor and Core Competency of Wise People*. In: R.J. Sternberg & J. Gluck [Eds.]. The Cambridge Handbook of Wisdom. Cambridge.
18. Stacey, R. (2012). *Tools and Techniques of Leadership and Management. Meeting the Challenge of Complexity*. Routledge.
19. Stacey, R. (2012). *Tools and Techniques of Leadership and Management. Meeting the Challenge of Complexity*. Routledge.
20. Levitt, H. (1999). The Development of Wisdom: An Analysis of Tibetan Buddhist Experience. *Journal of Humanistic Psychology*, 39(2), 86–105.
21. Edmondson, R. & Woerner, M.H. (2019). Sociocultural Foundations of Wisdom. In: R.J. Sternberg & J. Gluck [Eds.]. *The Cambridge Handbook of Wisdom*. Cambridge.

Part Two

Know Yourselves

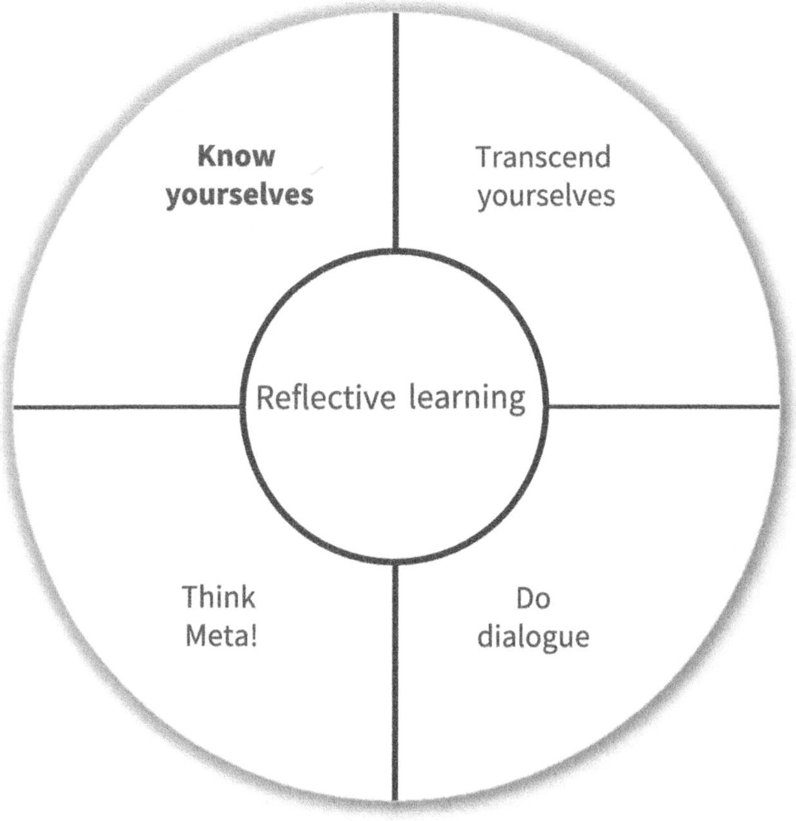

DOI: 10.4324/9781003284826-3

A leadership myth

Authenticity is About Honouring Your One True Self

Susan was invited to undertake a multi-rater 360° survey by her line manager. A coach from outside the organization, Will, was asked to show her the results and help her come up with a plan to move forward.

The survey showed how she was perceived by a variety of audiences, including direct reports, peers, and her line manager. It also showed how she was perceived by selected members of her friends and family. The results suggested that she was showing up as caring, confident, and supportive with family and friends. Her direct reports experienced her as more task-oriented, still caring, but somewhat reticent in meetings with people more senior to her if the subject matter was sensitive. Peers also experienced her as task focussed, but somewhat difficult to get to know. Her line manager experienced her as disciplined and committed, but reluctant to have hard conversations with colleagues.

Susan's coach invited her to reflect on how and why different people were seeing her behave differently in different contexts. He was particularly struck by how different she was showing up at home with friends and family than she was with colleagues at work. He suggested that there may be some anxiety and self-doubt at play preventing her from being her authentic self at work. He suggested they focus on helping her to define her authentic self, and then identify some of the factors in the workplace that might be stopping her from being that self at work. Susan left the meeting feeling somewhat inauthentic but looking forward to discovering who her authentic self might be and how she could bring that one true self to bear in every aspect of her life.

Susan may be able to find new levels of authenticity, but not by following the path advocated by her coach. Her coach has encouraged her to define a single true self, a self that shows up in every situation. A single self, free of anxiety and self-doubt. But an alternative interpretation of her results suggests that she is feeling pulled in different directions by different parts of herself. Anxiety and self-doubt are parts of her that want to be understood and recognized. They won't be pushed away. This idea that we should all aspire to be this one, true, authentic self is a myth. To become a great leader, so the story goes, a manager must develop a deeper understanding of their 'true' self, and then behave in accordance with that self at all times. The problem with this narrative is that there is little, if any, evidence to suggest we have one single true self. We have multiple selves. In this section, we outline an alternative meaning of the word authenticity and its implication for leadership.

Theory

We learned in Part One that an effective commitment to reflective learning includes a commitment to better understanding ourselves. The wisdom literature tells us that self-awareness is a key aspect of wisdom, and that wise people are more likely to question their intuitions[1]. The literature tells us also that wise leaders stay calm. They understand their emotions and can regulate their emotions effectively.

This is all useful but is usually couched in terms of a search for a single authentic self. We talk about ourselves as if we are one single person, thinking and behaving the same way in all circumstances. We worry if we find ourselves being perceived differently by different people in different situations – are we being authentic? This perspective of authenticity assumes we have one single self and the quest for authenticity is to find that self. But the evidence suggests we are not one, we are many. There is little evidence to support the notion of a single authentic self. That argument *'stands on rather weak feet'*[2]. This has implications both for how we think about self-awareness and authenticity. In this section, we talk about *selves-awareness*, an approach that implies a different understanding of what it means to be authentic.

As we talk about the idea of different selves, it is important to note that we are not talking about entirely independent selves. Theories of dissociative identity disorder point to the existence of different selves with segregated memory systems. If different selves have different memory systems, then a person can be unaware of what they have just been thinking, saying, or doing for the last few hours because those memories are exclusive to the self that was just running the show. This is like Dr Jekyll waking up in the morning blissfully unaware of what Mr Hyde got up to the night before. We are not talking about dissociative identity disorder here, a state often associated with a violent or abusive childhood and the need to compartmentalize experiences. We are talking about multiplicity as an entirely normal state of being. In this normal state of being our different selves share memories and experiences and they work together, sometimes effectively and other times less so.

Our premise is that wise leaders have great selves-awareness. If we are not one, but many, then we must explore who we are through a multiplicity lens if we are to become wiser. Delving into our multiplicity of self provides us with a much richer, deeper understanding of who we are and how we operate. It helps us understand why we show up differently in different situations. It helps us understand why we may feel a lack of confidence in new roles. It helps us understand why we sometimes experience inner tensions, being pulled in different directions by different parts of our selves. It helps us to appreciate the value of getting to know those parts of our selves we may not always value, instead of trying to push them away.

This perspective on self leads us to a very different view of authenticity. Authenticity, through this lens, is about the extent to which our different selves are aware of each other and work together collaboratively. Dr. Mary Watkins, a clinical and developmental psychologist, says that one aspect of healthy psychological development is the progressive elaboration of different internal characters, and the continuous enhancement of imaginary conversations between those characters[3]. Professor Tatiana Bachkirova distinguishes between the mature ego and the immature ego, our place on the scale depending on the extent to which all our various selves work effectively together[4]. Our task, therefore, is to first seek to understand our different selves, and then to learn how they might work together more effectively. As we will reflect upon later, Susan's 360° results present her with an opportunity to get to know some of her different selves, to embrace them all, and to help them embrace each other.

This is a perspective of self that invites us to acknowledge and be comfortable with inner tensions, ambivalence, and paradox. From this perspective such tensions are inevitable and represent an opportunity to learn more about one's selves. In contrast to the traditional perspective on self that encourages us to bet the house on a single self and push all the others away. That approach is not useful because in pushing the other selves away we forgo the opportunity to understand all our selves better and to become more authentic. The authentic multiple self is better able to manage complexity. As Karl Weick said, '*the more selves I have access to, the more meanings I should be able to extract and impose in any situation. The less likelihood I will find myself surprised*'[5].

The multiplicity perspective offers us another very different and important perspective on wisdom. Think back to our straw poll on the wisdom that we referred to in the introduction. You may recall that about half the people we surveyed said they had never worked for a wise leader. A much smaller minority said they had worked for several wise leaders. The first perspective is consistent with general findings. This perfectionist perspective on wisdom makes it less likely we can ever achieve wisdom – it is set up as an unattainable standard[6]. The multiplicity perspective encourages us to identify those *parts* of ourselves that are wise. Through this lens all of us are wise, in some respects. Through this lens there are lots of role models for us to learn from. We don't need to seek out the God-like guru, instead we can seek out aspects of wisdom from everyone with whom we interact and from within our selves. Again, this multiplicity perspective may have good evidence to support it. Research suggests people are wise in some contexts and not in others[7]. Is this perhaps because different parts of ourselves are more present in some situations than in others?

In this section, we will briefly consider the evidence for multiplicity and the origins of multiplicity. As we will see, the evidence for some form of multiplicity is quite compelling, and you may be surprised by how old some multiplicity theories are. There are so many theories, some quite different from each other and we highlight a few of those differences.

Evidence for multiplicity

In 1983, Benjamin Libet and colleagues wired up six people, measuring readiness-to-act and the appearance of conscious intention[8]. They found that readiness-to-act preceded conscious intention by several hundred milliseconds. In other words, a part of the brain initiated an action before the conscious part of the brain was aware the decision had been made. This suggests that there is an unconscious part of the brain that makes certain decisions without us being aware.

Making up a story to explain something we are unsure about is called confabulation. Michael Gazzaniga and colleagues showed this confabulation in action[9]. They worked with split-brain patients. A split-brain patient has all the connections between left and right half of the brain severed, often to help patients better manage epilepsy. Gazzaniga set up screens so that he could show pictures to the left and right hemispheres of the brain separately (Figure 2.1).

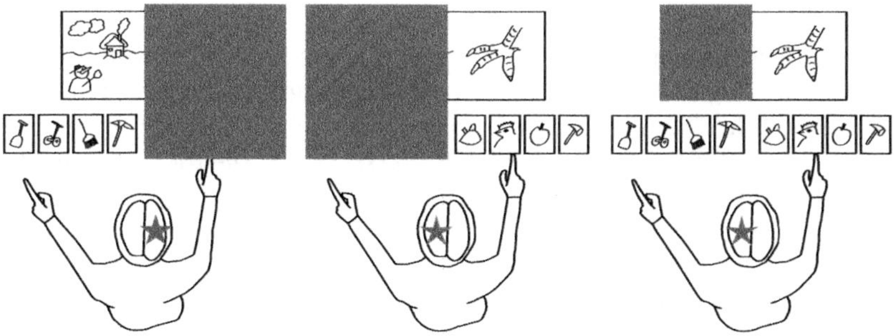

The RHS of the brain sees the snowdrift and picks the shovel.

The LHS of the brain sees the chicken foot and and picks the chicken head.

The patient is asked why they chose the shovel. The LHS of the brain is the part that is conscious and speaks. It can't see what the RHS of the brain sees – and confabulates e.g. *"I picked the shovel to clean the chicken shed."*

Figure 2.1 Gazzaniga's experiments with split-brain patients.

He and his team showed each hemisphere a picture and asked each hemisphere to indicate, non-verbally – by pointing, which of four smaller pictures best related to that big picture. For example, they showed the right hemisphere of a patient's brain a picture of a snowstorm and the patient correctly pointed to a shovel. They showed the left hemisphere of the brain a picture of a chicken's foot and the patient correctly pointed to a chicken's head.

The researchers then asked patients, *verbally*, why they made their selections. Patients typically said that they chose the chicken's head because they saw a chicken's foot. So far, so good – the left hemisphere of the brain knew why it made the choice it did and was able to explain its choice, since this the left hemisphere is conscious and has a voice.

However, when the researchers asked patients why they chose the shovel, they made up stories, because only the left-hand side of the brain has conscious choice and the capacity to explain its decisions. It was the *right-hand* side of the brain that chose the shovel (correctly - because it saw the snowstorm). But the left hemisphere of the brain hadn't seen the snowstorm, nor was it able to communicate with the right-hand side of the brain because the left- and right-hand sides of the brain were now divided. But we don't understand this about ourselves and so the left-hand brain felt compelled to answer the question, to confabulate. Some patients said, for example, that they chose the shovel to clean out a chicken shed.

How should we interpret these findings? It seems that there are parts of our selves located in the right-hand side of the brain interacting with the environment and making decisions, separate from the parts of our selves on the left-hand side of the brain that also interact with the environment and makes decisions. As we have explained, the left-hand side of the brain is conscious and has the capacity to speak and thinks it is the only part of the brain making decisions. Gazzaniga and colleagues called this part of the left-brain the left-hemisphere-interpreter. The right-hand side of the brain has no voice, but normally feeds its perspectives silently into the left-hemisphere interpreter.

These findings imply that in those of us with intact brains, with left- and right-hand sides of the brain connected, there are different parts of ourselves located in different parts of the brain, independently making decisions, and making sense of the world. Some parts of our brain are conscious and have the capacity to voice, but other parts of the brain are not fully conscious, nor do they have the capacity to voice what they are experiencing. Those parts of the brain, including the right hemisphere, communicate silently to the left-hemisphere interpreter, which then adds those voices to its observations, thoughts, and feelings without knowing what has happened. On this basis, Gazzaniga and colleagues argued that our 'self' isn't a single brain function located in one part of the brain. Rather it is multi-faceted, distributed across different parts of the brain.

If you remain unconvinced, ask yourself:

- Do you ever find yourself talking to yourself? Especially when making hard decisions. If so – who is talking to who?
- Do you ever hear yourself referring to yourself as 'we' instead of 'I'? if so – who are 'we'?
- Do you ever look back and wonder why you said something or behaved in a certain way? Who is reflecting on who's behaviour?

We said that most of us relate to being a single self and talk about ourselves as a single entity with a single set of values and beliefs. Yet the idea of multiplicity *also* makes sense to most of us. In experiments with students, various researchers have shown that most people identify somewhere between three and nine different selves[10].

A short history of multiplicity

Plato was born four hundred years BC. He believed that the soul gave life to the body and that the soul is that part of us which thinks. Plato's soul comprised three parts, each residing in a different part of the body. According to Plato, the *logos* is located in the head and is related to reason. The logos also regulates the other parts of the soul. The *thymos* is located near the chest and relates to spirit. The *eros* is located in the stomach and is related to desire. Reason, desire, and spirit are often in conflict. Plato wrote about the good horse (spirit) and the bad horse (desire) pulling into two different directions, ultimately being steered by the charioteer (reason).

We can see shadows of Plato's tripartite soul in the writings of Sigmund Freud. Freud described the psyche rather than the soul. Freud also wrote about horses. In his analogy, the *id* is the horse, a set of uncoordinated instinctual desires. The *ego* is the rider, seeking to channel the power of the id in a particular direction. The id is the source of bodily needs and wants, emotional impulses and desires, including aggression and the sex drive. The ego is reasonable and goal focussed, a bit like Plato's reason interacting with Plato's desire. The ego incorporates conscious awareness, though not every part of the ego is conscious. The *super-ego* reflects the internalization of rules from other people and seeks to behave in ways deemed to be socially appropriate. The super-ego acts as our conscience and operates mostly unconsciously.

There exist multiple contemporary multiplicity theories. John Rowan writes about different 'subpersonalities'[11]. These different sub-personalities may be specific to the individual and not generic. They are dynamic and they evolve. Richard Schwartz writes about different 'parts' of the selfexisting alongside a 'core self'[12]. When parts work against each other the person feels fragmented. Schwartz suggests that all parts are valuable and well-intended. They want to play constructive inner roles, in a system in which the core self is able to play a leadership role. Rita Carter compares the mind to a physical landscape, with personalities constantly forming, evolving, and fading away[13]. The landscape changes rapidly in younger people but settles down over the years. A typical profile consists of one or two 'majors', several 'minors' and any number of 'micros'. Micros may combine to form minors, and minors may coalesce to form majors. Unlike Rowan and Schwartz, David Lester does not necessarily believe in the existence of a single over-arching executive self. Where multiple selves exist, at any point in time, one subself is in control of the mind, and other subselves are suspended. Some of the suspended selves may be monitoring what the executive subself is up to, while others may not. Allen McConnell suggests that the individual's overall self-concept comprises self-aspects that form in response to goals and motivations[14]. Each self-aspect is composed of attributes, which are not necessarily specific to any one self-aspect. Tatiana Bachkirova suggests there exist three aspects of self[15]. First, the pre-reflective sense of self, a primitive, inarticulate entity that distinguishes between self and non-self. The second aspect of self is the 'ego', a network of numerous mini-selves that translate the needs and functions of an individual into action. Some of these mini-selves are part of the conscious mind, while others form part of the unconscious mind. Some are simple, others are more complex. They may engage with each other and occasionally conflict. The third aspect of self is the narrator, a linguistic function consistent with that suggested by Gazzaniga[16]. The role of the narrator is to make up a story that explains how the organism as a whole interacts with its environment. This story is ultimately fictitious, since the narrator does not have access to what is happening in the unconscious and may or may not reflect the nature of the sub-selves.

Differences between theories

Language

Some writers refer to different selves, identities, sub-personalities, sub-systems, parts etc …

If the multiple perspective on self is interesting to you, we encourage you to find a language that works best for you in describing your different selves. You can call them; selves, identities, voices, parts, aspects, sub-personalities – whatever you like, but we encourage you to call them something. Some descriptors are a bit academic, referring directly to underlying theory, while Schwartz refer to 'parts' because he says this is the language most of us use. For example, a part of me thinks this, a part of me thinks that … Decide what makes sense to you.

In doing so, it's important to note that we're not just talking about different preferences or different moods. I might like both the idea of eating chocolate and the idea of not eating chocolate. Each part of me may also like the idea of eating chocolate and not eating chocolate. Multiplicity theory comes into play when we notice that there are some circumstances when we don't hesitate to eat chocolate, lots of it, and there are circumstances where we find it easy to resist eating chocolate. Then this isn't simply a case of competing preferences – something else is going on to determine our desire for chocolate in the moment.

Nor are we talking only about mood. My different selves may display certain emotions more than others, but I usually have more than one self that leans toward a particular emotion, and most of my selves experience more than one emotion. Each of our selves has its own emotional repertoire. If I am feeling very happy today, it doesn't necessarily mean that my very happy self is at play. It may mean that one of my selves that can feel happy, is at play.

Generic or specific types?

Writers also differ in the extent they believe we all have the same or similar portfolio of selves. Eric Berne described parent, adult, and child selves[17]. Rita Carter suggests there exist common archetypes[18]. For example, guardians who alert us to danger, worriers who imagine the worst, pleasers who want us to be on the good side of people, fighters who hit out against threats, controllers, drivers, organizers, punishers, bullies, etc.

Other writers think more in terms of sources specific to the individual. Through this lens, our portfolio of selves is more fluid and dynamic. For example, becoming a sibling, becoming a parent, or assuming a leadership position can evoke a new self. Our research has highlighted the various ways in which people come to see themselves as a leader, and how this process can be accelerated or derailed depending on how easy it is for us to access a leadership self[19]. Our leader selves form, and reform, representing just one of many selves we may identify with. We may internalize heroes and heroines, including famous people and people who we admire in our lives. Our parents often show up in one or more of our inner selves.

Later in this section, we invite you to think about your different selves with reference to a generic list of possible selves or to just make up your own selves 'bottom-up' and see what emerges. There is no right or wrong when it comes to identifying your list of possible selves.

Narrator or not?

Plato wrote about *reason*, the charioteer, seeking to manage the good and bad horses of spirit and desire. Freud wrote about the *ego*, within which resides consciousness. Schwartz writes about the *Self*, interacting successfully or otherwise with the parts. Tatiana Bachkirova's describes the *narrator*, making up stories to explain how the person as a whole interacts with the environment. Bachkirova's narrator reminds us of Plato's reason and Gazzaniga's

Left Hemisphere Interpreter. The narrator is the part of ourselves that makes sense of it all. Many of the stories told by the narrator are made up because the narrator does not have access to what is happening in the subconscious. The narrator confabulates, just as the Left-Hemisphere Interpreter confabulates. Not all writers agree that there is an executive function, however. Some writers suggest that at any one time, one self is leading the way. When a new self steps up, then the old self steps down.

Which interpretation intuitively makes the most sense to you?

The value of a multiple perspective – case study

We coached Bob. Bob was a senior executive who came looking for coaching. Bob had risen quickly through the ranks at BigPharma. He had been working for BigPharma for 18 months before the assignment began. He joined as an account manager and within 12 months was promoted into a business development role with a place on the senior leadership team reporting to the CEO. In his new role he led two teams and was responsible for building a new business model for a key market segment. The organization loved his enthusiasm and creativity. But the senior executive team were finding him hard to work with. At every meeting, he would present his ideas with great energy and passion, but people found it hard to follow what he was saying. At the end of a pitch, he would tell colleagues what he planned to do next, but by the next meeting, his plans had changed. Other teams were getting fed up with him. It was hard for them to build their own plans when Bob kept moving the goalposts without telling anyone.

Talking through the situation with his coach, Bob explained how he yearned to be able to express himself more clearly, and how he was constantly derailed by the effort it took in the moment to manage *'a thousand thoughts down to five'*. Having a thousand thoughts in his head at any one time made it difficult to present a focussed message. It wasn't that Bob couldn't prioritize and organize his thoughts – it was that he didn't want to bring too much structure into his thinking for fear that would compromise his spontaneity and creativity.

As Bob and his coach talked, two aspects of Bob's self emerged. The first was a desire to be creative and the second was a desire to be more organized, aspects that were in conflict. His coach asked Bob to give character to both these aspects of self. Bob characterized the first self as the 'Mad Professor'. The Mad Professor (MP) was 'sunshine yellow', bringing to Bob outside-the-box thinking, energy, humour, and a capacity to join the dots. The MP was male, dressed in red swimming trunks and goggles. Bob's second self was the 'Aggressive Librarian'. The Aggressive Librarian (AL) was red and blue and dressed in a suit. The AL was grounded and driven, focussed on process and information. He was the nay-sayer who wants to run the show but didn't because he feels untrusted, unskilled, and tired. Trying to talk to the MP exhausted him.

As they talked Bob came to realize that his executive team wanted to reap the benefits of MP's work whilst spending most of their time interacting with AL. But the MP had more energy than AL and basically ran the show all the time. As the assignment progressed, Bob became clearer as to the qualities that the MP and the AL each brought to the table and the risks of allowing the MP to dominate. He sought to understand how to bring the right balance of each to different contexts. He tried getting AL and the MP to start talking to each other, to see if they might find a better way of working together.

After a few sessions, Bob and his coach engaged with the CEO. The CEO offered Bob a lot of affirming feedback, commending Bob essentially on the MP's qualities ('*You're an amazing guy, energetic and dynamic*'), while making the case for more input from AL ('*All I'm looking for is the delivery*'). Over the next few months, Bob made great strides in his capacity to prioritize and organize. He shared the idea of the MP and AL with his team, asking them to let him know when the MP was in charge and out of control. Bob and his coach used further sessions to review specific incidents to further reflect on how the MP and AL interacted and how they could work together better.

Authenticity and learning to dance

The task of becoming more authentic through this lens has two stages to it. First, seek to understand each aspect of self. Second, help those different selves to get to know each other better and to work together more collaboratively - to learn to dance with one another. Bob solved his issues when the MP and the AL learned to work together. Richard Schwartz writes about the dynamics between our different inner selves[20]. He encourages us to get to know our different 'parts' and to help those parts achieve balance. He suggests it is useful to think of our different parts as different (but related) people, of different ages and backgrounds, but all committed to being helpful. When the parts are working well together, the person doesn't experience each part distinctly and feels quite unitary. Sometimes the parts become imbalanced or polarised and the parts must learn to collaborate more effectively if balance is to be restored. Through this lens, the wise person experiences balance, a calmness borne of her different selves having learned to collaborate and cooperate more effectively. Our selves have effectively learned how to dance together.

Becoming more aware of our emotions

Not everyone includes emotions in their definitions of wisdom[21]. Some do. The HERO(E) Model, for example, defines wisdom in terms of humour, *emotional regulation*, reflectiveness, openness, and life experience[22]. The MORE Life Experience Model talks about mastery, openness, reflectivity, and *emotional competence*[23]. Becoming more emotionally competent starts with paying attention to our emotions and learning more about ourselves through that reflection. Becoming more emotionally competent starts, therefore, with coming more selves-aware. This requires us to get to know our emotions, even those we don't much like.

The wisdom literature tells us that wise leaders relate appropriately to conflicting emotions without repressing them[24]. It tells us that wise people are sensitive to the feelings of others, and to their own emotions. They are tolerant of unwanted emotions. They neither seek to suppress those emotions, nor do they linger too long. Paying attention to those emotions enables them to better manage their emotions over time[25]. A multiplicity lens inspires us to bring their emotions closer rather than push them away. If I feel angry or anxious, for example, what are the voices in my head telling me at that moment? What values are being challenged? What fears are being evoked? Which of my selves appear to be being triggered? Why have those selves shown up in the moment? And what conversations need to be had among those selves?

In Part Five, 'Do Dialogue', we will talk about what is meant by 'speak from the I'. To 'speak from the I' effectively requires us to *think* from the 'I'. To *think* from the 'I' requires us to be aware of the inner voices that fill our head with thoughts, often judgmental thoughts. We need to understand them if we are to be able to behave independent of those thoughts. And so our exploration of our multiple selves must include a consideration of their emotions. How do each of my selves feel in what contexts, and what thoughts are driving each set of emotions in each situation?

In this section, we have introduced the idea of multiplicity. Knowing those different selves, however, often isn't enough. We need not only to understand our different selves, but we need to understand where they came from. We need to understand our own growth in terms of a collective capacity to learn. This is the symbiotic positivity principle again. In Part Three we will further develop our understanding of sources of self, all in service of becoming wiser.

Epilogue

Susan Goes Multiple

Susan was invited to undertake a multi-rater 360° survey by her line manager. A coach from outside the organization, Dan, was asked to show her the results and help her come up with a plan to move forward.

The survey showed how she was perceived by a variety of audiences, including direct reports, peers, her line manager, friends, and family. The results suggested that she was showing up as caring, confident, and supportive with family and friends. Her direct reports experienced her as more task oriented. Peers also experienced her as task focussed, but somewhat difficult to get to know. Her line manager experienced her as disciplined and committed, but reluctant to have hard conversations with colleagues.

Dan invited Susan to reflect on how and why different people were seeing her behave differently in different contexts. He was particularly struck at how different she was showing up at home, with friends and family, than she was with colleagues at work. He invited her to characterize those different selves.

Susan noticed how her caring-self was always to the fore with family and friends. In that environment, she felt less urge to get things done and focussed more on people and how they were feeling. Her caring-self showed up also with direct reports but was accompanied by her doing-self. When engaging with direct reports, caring-self, and doing-self worked together reasonably well to achieve a balance of camaraderie and productivity.

With peers, caring-self left more space for doing-self. Caring-self didn't think that her peers needed her attention – her peers all seemed so focused and confident and in a hurry. When it came to having difficult conversations with peers, caring-self's reticence encouraged self-doubting-self to step up and make sure that she said nothing to colleagues that might result in those colleagues becoming angry or sad – she didn't want to jeopardize any of those relationships.

She recognized how caring-self and doing-self worked together less effectively when in the presence of senior leaders. In that context, caring-self became overly attentive to cues suggesting she wasn't doing a good job. That encouraged self-doubting-self to step in, to make sure she didn't say anything controversial and that she played it safe. The arrival of self-doubting-self intimidated doing-self, who spoke only when permitted to do so by self-doubting-self.

Susan wondered how she might be more courageous in conversations with peers and senior colleagues. She reflected on those times in her life when she did speak out. She recalled conversations with the teachers at her child's school when he had complained of being bullied. She recalled times when it felt like her values were being challenged at work, when she absolutely did speak up to whoever was around, no matter their role in the organization. She drew forth her courageous-self and thought about some of her interactions with peers and senior leaders through that lens. Her courageous-self was a few years older than her, indeed looked a bit like one of her favourite aunts, a woman who always seemed confident and in control, who brooked no nonsense with anyone.

Susan found this approach to feedback much more useful than previous experiences, but still somewhat confusing. This analysis suggested that she showed up in one particular way with each particular audience. But she knew that wasn't true, her family and friends gave her feedback outside this process that she sometimes showed up loving and caring, other times grumpy and withdrawn. And what about when she was dealing with multiple audiences? There were plenty of occasions when she was interacting both with peers and direct reports, or peers and senior leaders, or senior leaders and direct reports. Dan encouraged Susan to go and talk to her raters, ask more questions about how they perceived her and in what scenarios. As she spoke to people Susan became clearer as to how she showed up in different roles and different scenarios, and how her different selves were working together.

Before her next presentation to senior leadership, which she delivered with two members of her team, she imagined her courageous-self telling her to, '*just say what needs to be said*' and her caring-self saying, '*support your team and connect with the audience. Find out what they need*'. After the presentation her two team members looked at her with newfound admiration. They said she seemed so confident, so clear in what she said, yet also open for discussion. The senior leaders in the room enjoyed the conversation, assured that she knew what she was talking about, and happy to give her the space to progress her team's agenda.

Self-development

The multiplicity approach acknowledges that we are complex beings, full of different energies and motivations that can at times pull us in all different directions. It isn't helpful to try and over-simplify our perception of self, to try and reduce ourselves to one set of energies and motivations. This is to leave the task of self-discovery largely undone. The multiplicity perspective is to acknowledge our complexity and provide one means by which to explore it. The first thing we encourage you to do in terms of self-development is to decide where you sit on the whole topic. If it does seem useful to you, then think about the questions we asked you earlier:

- What language will you use to define your different selves?
- Will you seek to identify your own selves or will you leverage someone else's generic typology?
- Do your different selves take turns running the show, or is there a narrator-self overseeing things?

Consider, when did you last became frustrated or annoyed with someone and allowed that annoyance to show up in your behaviour. How might you have behaved differently had you:

- Been more familiar with your 'impatient self' or whatever you choose to call it?
- Understood what triggered your impatient self into action?
- Been more aware of your other selves, for example, an 'empathic self'?
- Been able to give more space to your empathic self, such that your empathic self was able to agree with your impatient self how best to approach the conversation?

In this section, we outline a methodology to help you identify your different selves and to help them work together more collaboratively. In building this process we draw upon the work of some other writers. Rita Carter, for example, describes a structured approach that combines considering ten aspects of personality with thinking about specific roles you play in life[26]. She invites you to think about those roles, one by one, and to characterize them in terms of whether each of the ten personality types is present or absent, and then in terms of sub-markers for each of the personality domains. John Rowan outlines six sources of sub-personality and invites us to consider the different roles that we play and the conflicts that arise between some of those selves[27]. Our methodology leverages some of Carter and Rowan's ideas and other writers too. It comprises six steps:

1 Listing the different roles that you play in life – e.g., parent, friend, leader, etc. …
2 Characterizing 'you' in each of those roles
3 Identifying how many different selves are present across those roles
4 Testing your hypothesis
5 Reflecting on any tensions between these selves
6 Learning to dance

First time around you may seek to complete all these exercises quickly in search of immediate insights. By all means, play with the exercises as you will. In our experience, however, the most meaningful insights come from ongoing reflection on how we experience dilemma. Each time we make time to reflect helps us become more selves aware and helps us to become wiser.

Step one – the roles that you play

List all the different roles you play in life. Don't worry how many roles you come up with – some people name 5 or 6 roles, others many more.

Shaun listed all the roles he thinks he plays in life. He identified 15 roles (Table 2.1).

Step two – characterize self in each role

For each of the roles you have come up with, ask yourself questions like:

1 What emotions do you experience in each of these roles?
2 What behaviours?
3 What drives each of these personas?

Table 2.1 Shaun's 15 roles

Loving partner	Loving parent	Considerate line manager
Action-oriented partner	Loyal friend	Considerate line manager
Playful partner	Mischievous friend	Demanding line manager
Rule enforcing parent	Supportive peer at work	Acquiescent subordinate
Playful parent	Busy peer	Rebel subordinate

4 What sort of thing does each of these personas tend to say?
5 What age/appearance is each of these personas?

We invite you to fully characterize each of your personas so that they become really clear for you. Think back to Bob. Bob identified two parts of himself – his creative self and his grounded, driven self. Giving full character to each of these selves turned something fuzzy and conceptual into something real and tangible. His creative self became the 'Mad Professor', a 'sunshine yellow' self, dressed in swimmers and goggles. Bob's driven self was red and blue and dressed in a suit. He was often grumpy and tired.

Bringing character to your different selves helps you to differentiate between them, recognize when they are present, understand what they need and how they are likely to behave. Ultimately bringing character to your different selves helps you manage them more effectively.

Shaun worked through the process for each role (Table 2.2).

Step three – refine yourselves

A role is not the same as a self. For example, Shaun looks across the different personas he has created for each role, and notices that several of those personas are similar or the same. For example, the action-oriented partner, the rule-enforcing parent, the demanding line manager; they all seem very determined, very focussed, very outcome focussed. You too will probably see lots of repetition across the different roles you listed. This is because your different selves show up in several roles. Now look across all the roles that you play and look for commonalities. Those commonalities represent your different 'selves'. Most people identify somewhere between 3 and 9 different selves.

Shaun looks at his table and distilled six different selves (Table 2.3).

Shaun went a step further in characterizing his six selves and drew pictures. This helped him better explore the different selves he identified (Figure 2.2).

As Shaun reflected on each of his different selves, he started to feel more authentic. Naming each of his selves helps him begin to understand some of the internal tensions he experienced when feeling uncertain or uneasy. It helped him understand why he showed up differently in different scenarios. He felt lighter, realizing it is OK to show up differently to different people in different contexts, as long as he understands what is going on.

Step four – test your hypotheses

You can enact this stage in the process at any time once you've done at least some initial work. Now it's time to take a deep breath. Your self-analysis so far is all hypothetical and based on how you experience yourself. But what sense do your nearest and dearest make of your hypotheses? That might be people at home, friends, or people at work. Just pick people you trust. Ask them how

Table 2.2 Shaun's 15 roles and different personas

Role	*Age/appearance*	*Behaviours*	*Emotions*	*Drivers*	*Says things like …*
Loving partner	50 s – me now. Dressed casual.	Attentive Loving	Love Compassion	Support Nurture	'What are you thinking?'
Action-oriented partner	30 s – short hair. Gym gear	Focused Single-minded	Calm Determination	Action Resolve	'This is what we need to do'.
Playful partner	20 s – untidy/unshaven	Spontaneous Intimate	Joy Happiness	Connection Have fun	'Go for it!'
Rule enforcing parent	40 s – casual clothes	Strict Stern	Determination	Maintain order	'I want you to …'
Playful parent	20 s – untidy/ruffled hair	Attentive Loving	Joy Happiness	Connection Have fun	'Have a go!'
Loving parent	40 s – casual clothes	Attentive Loving	Love Compassion	Support Nurture	'What are you thinking?'
Loyal friend	50 s – casual	Available Supportive	Love Determination	Support Nurture	'What can I do to help?'
Mischievous friend	30 s – untidy/ruffled hair	Spontaneous Playful	Joy Happiness	Have fun	"Have you heard the one about?"
Supportive peer	40 s – work clothes	Sociable Engaging	Empathy Consideration	Collaboration	'How are you today?'
Busy peer	40 s – work clothes. Ruffled.	Hurried Distracted	Intentional Anxious	Learn	'Not now …'
Considerate line manager	40 s – work clothes	Sociable Engaging	Empathy Respect	Collaboration Support	'How are you today?'
Demanding line manager	40 s – suit & shirt well pressed	Stern Focussed	Determination Impatient	Achieve	'This is what I need'.
Acquiescent subordinate	Child. Smart clothes.	Attentive Compliant	Connection Attachment	Harmony	'What do you need?'
Rebel subordinate	Teens. Jeans & trainers	Strict Unbending	Determination Impatient	Resolve	'No'.
Caring subordinate	40 s – work clothes	Sociable Caring	Empathy Concern	Collaboration Support	'How can I help?'

Table 2.3 Shaun's six selves

Self	*Age/appearance*	*Behaviours*	*Emotions*	*Drivers*	*Says things like …*
Action Shaun Representing *action-oriented partner, rule enforcing parent,* and *demanding line manager*	40 s – short hair/ sharply dressed/ clean shaven	Focussed Unbending Impatient	Determination Focus Impatient	Achieve	'Let's do it'.
Playful Shaun Representing etc …	20 s – jeans, trainers, scruffy	Spontaneous Playful Intimate Doing it!	Joy Happiness Love Bounce Drive	Have fun Progression Health Vitality	'Let's just try it?'
Loving Shaun	50 s – casual clothes	Attentive Loving Sociable Engaging Supportive	Love Compassion Empathy Determination Respect Happiness	Support Nurture Collaboration	'How are you feeling?'
Focussed Shaun	50 s – smart casual	Thinking Serene	Calm Thoughtful Intentional Quiet	Learn	'What's going on here?'
Contrary Shaun	Teens – dressed to offend!	Challenging	Energetic	Justice	'I don't agree'.
Self-critical Shaun	Child – smart clothes	Attentive Compliant	Connection Self-doubt Anxiety	Harmony	To self: 'What are you doing wrong?'

Figure 2.2 Shaun's six selves.

they experience your different selves. Do they recognize them all? In what circumstances do they see them show up? Be curious about listening to their feedback. Their feedback will help you understand how your different selves are co-created in relationships with others – the theme of the next mantra.

Step five – reflect on inner tension

Every time we experience inner conflict is an opportunity to further explore our inner selves. Our action is to make the time to reflect on inner conflict every time we experience it and to consciously learn from those reflections. This is an ongoing, never-ending journey, but the more effort we allocate to that process, the more self-aware we become, and the wiser we become.

For example, a colleague asked Shaun if he was free that evening to have a conversation about a decision he was struggling to make regarding his career. Shaun wanted to help his colleague (Loving Shaun) but had already made plans to go and enjoy himself at the pub that Friday night with friends (Playful Shaun). What did Shaun do? By consciously tapping into Focused Shaun, he gained greater clarity on the tensions he was experiencing. He realized the tension was sitting between Loving Shaun and Playful Shaun and worked out a way forward that satisfied both. He set an hour aside straight after work to talk to his colleague to be a sounding board before arriving a bit late to be with his friends. Reflecting on his reflection, he learned that Focused Shaun was that part of himself that was best at playing the role of mediator. He resolved to bring Focused Shaun to the fore more often, by asking reflective questions of himself as soon as he noticed tension within himself. The next time he felt tense,

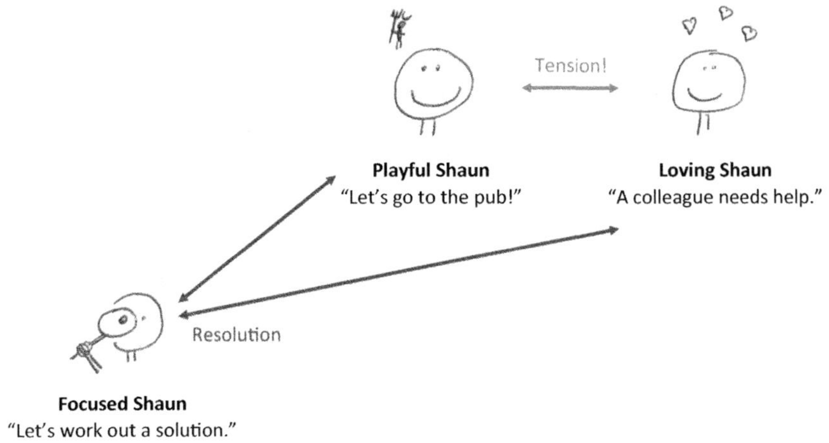

Figure 2.3 Resolving tension.

instead of carrying that tension around with him all day, he would ask Focused Shaun – '*What's going on? Who needs to talk to who?*' (Figure 2.3).

Step six – learn to dance

Consciously reflecting on our different selves and building the capacity to bring them purposefully to bear in different contexts is a life-long endeavour. Managing internal conflict in the way that Shaun did takes time and practice. Our ability to do this well is grounded in our willingness to reflect on, and learn from, our experiences, and in our ongoing commitment to reflective learning.

Returning to our example we can see that Shaun has by now a pretty good hypothesis as to the nature of his various selves. Through his reflections, he is on the way to becoming more authentic. But remember, authenticity through this lens is not only about understanding the identity of our different selves, it's also about the extent to which our different selves are aware of each other and work together collaboratively. This may require purposeful exploration on our part. Not least because many texts encourage us to push away aspects of ourselves that we don't like – Rick Carson's book, *Taming Your Gremlin*, for example. Whilst there may be some circumstances in which this may be appropriate, it isn't the most useful strategy for most of us. For most of us, each of our selves has our best intentions at heart. If we are to become more authentic, we need to pull these selves toward us, not push them away. We need to understand their best intention and reflect as to how it may best be harnessed.

So, which way to go - push away or draw towards?

Shaun, for example, has identified Self-critical Shaun. Should he seek to push him away, to ignore self-doubt, and pretend he feels totally confident all the time? Or should he acknowledge Self-critical Shaun, seek to understand him and how best he might work with Shaun's other selves? Shaun decides to try the second option. Indeed, he seeks to understand how each of his selves can be helpful, at certain times and in certain contexts.

This was all new to Shaun and the task of exploring six selves in-depth felt daunting. He decided to start with the five selves that show up in a work scenario (Table 2.4).

Reviewing these selves helped Shaun make sense of feedback he had received in the past. For example, he had been told he needed to slow down and spend more time investing in relationships. This sounds like Action Shaun needing to give ground sometimes to Loving Shaun. Action Shaun didn't like ceding ground to Loving Shaun because whilst that seemed to help with team morale, others expressed dissatisfaction that he wasn't as productive as he used to be. This dissatisfaction prompted Self-critical Shaun to get worried.

He had also been told in the past that he got too carried away with new ideas (Playful Shaun), that he needed to learn how to translate good ideas into practical actions (Focused Shaun). He had tried taking this advice, but Playful Shaun became bored. Playful Shaun and Focused Shaun pulled in different directions. A coach debriefing him on the outcomes of a psychometric instrument warned him that an overabundance of creativity was likely to derail his career. But without that creativity, without making space for Playful Shaun, how could he be innovative and creative?

Shaun recognized that the feedback he received was often very polar – be this, and don't be this. This is often how feedback is delivered and/or how we choose to receive it. Again, it speaks to the idea that we have one self, that we somehow need to fine-tune this one self so that it behaves consistently and effectively in all scenarios. Through a multiplicity lens the world looked quite different to Shaun.

He realized that all five of these selves were useful and brought him value. The question wasn't – which of these selves are best and need to be cultivated, and which of these selves are worse and need to be obliterated? The more pertinent question was, *how might these selves all get to know each other better and learn to work together more effectively?* Shaun's challenge – the same challenge facing us all – is to recognize all the different aspects of his selves and to work out which selves to bring to any given scenario. Again, this is no easy feat, but doing the hard yards helps us make sense of all the different ways people experience us and we experience ourselves. By naming and recognizing our different selves we step closer to feeling authentic and being able to rise to the challenge of leading in today's complex world. So, while the task of getting to know your different selves is challenging, in our view it represents wisdom in action.

In considering how his selves worked together though, Shaun found he needed to think about specific contexts. He was pretty sure his different selves worked most effectively together differently, in different situations (Table 2.5).

Table 2.4 Shaun's five selves at work

Self	*Helps me to …*	*Stops me from …*	*Intention for me to …*	*Bring forth when …*
Action Shaun	Get things done	Getting bogged down. Stopping to think. Building relationships.	Be successful by being productive.	Things need to get done
Playful Shaun	Build relationships Innovate and create	Becoming morose. Being realistic	Be successful by building relationships and creating new stuff	We need to have fun and/or innovate
Loving Shaun	Connect with others	Losing connection. Making tough decisions	Be successful by building relationships	Needing to connect
Focused Shaun	Make good decisions Stop and think	Charging ahead willy-nilly	Make time to learn	Need time to think, grow and develop
Self-critical Shaun	Beware threats	Taking risks	Be successful by being prudent	The environment is uncertain

Table 2.5 Shaun's five work selves' contributions in different scenarios

	Having a difficult conversation	*Making a difficult decision*	*If over-used …*
Action Shaun	Voice own perspective clearly.	Maintain energy for being decisive	Forgets to listen – others become disengaged
Playful Shaun	Look for opportunities to lighten tension	Generate lots of options – not getting bogged down in one or two trains of thought	Loses focus on reality.
Loving Shaun	Stay tuned in to how the other person is feeling, responding appropriately.	Make sure people's needs are considered	Worries too much about how others are feeling – inertia.
Focused Shaun	Keep conversation on track. Observe what's happening. Ensure all the selves come in at the right time.	Create quiet time to think and reflect	Withdraws from engaging with others.
Self-critical Shaun	Monitor behaviour of other selves during conversation – speak out if things start not to go well	Keep quiet until after decision made. Make sure all selves review outcomes and reflect on those outcomes.	Becomes anxious and indecisive.

In his mind, Shaun began to see all his selves mingling together – before he had seen each as separate and isolated. He began to see their ongoing relationships as a complex dance. He watched them moving in and out of each other's way, sometimes gracefully, sometimes clumsily, and he determined to help them work together effectively. To do so he would need to check-in with them all regularly, reflect on their dynamic, how well they were working together, and how they could improve their dynamic. Thinking through the challenges he was facing as leader, he considered two situations to which he didn't always respond well:

1 Under time pressure

When under time pressure, Shaun recognized he tended to drive his team hard. Two team members had recently resigned, saying they felt tired and overwhelmed. Shaun visualized the dance his selves needed to engage in. He recognized that:

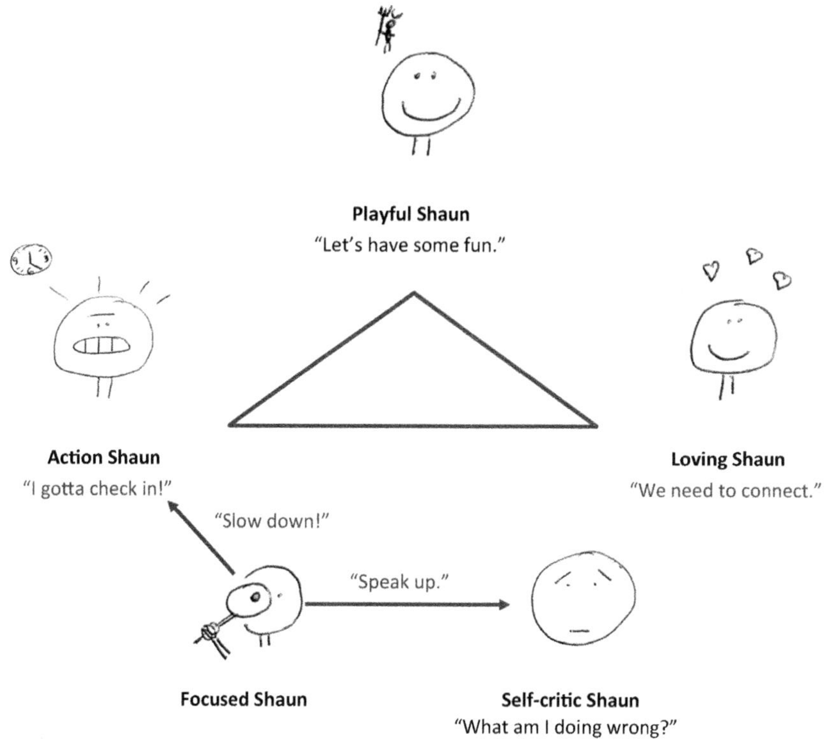

Figure 2.4 The time pressure dance.

- Action Shaun, Loving Shaun, and Playful Shaun needed to collaborate better in these scenarios. In driving to get things done, Action Shaun often forgot to check in with colleagues to understand what help they needed, and he became unrelentingly intense and serious. Action Shaun needed to take an occasional breath, step back, and create the space for Loving Shaun and Playful Shaun to connect.
- To enable this to happen, Focused Shaun needed to remind Action Shaun to slow down. Action Shaun needed to diarise reflection time and treat that reflection time as a task, like every other task, something to be achieved no matter what.
- During that reflection time, Focused Shaun needed to make sure Self-critical Shaun was heard. When Self-critical Shaun got anxious, he tended to push Action Shaun harder, to pay attention to the things he was neglecting (Figure 2.4).

2 Innovating

Playful Shaun loved to innovate and create. He became excited, which in turn got Action Shaun excited, and they could drive a group forward to commit to

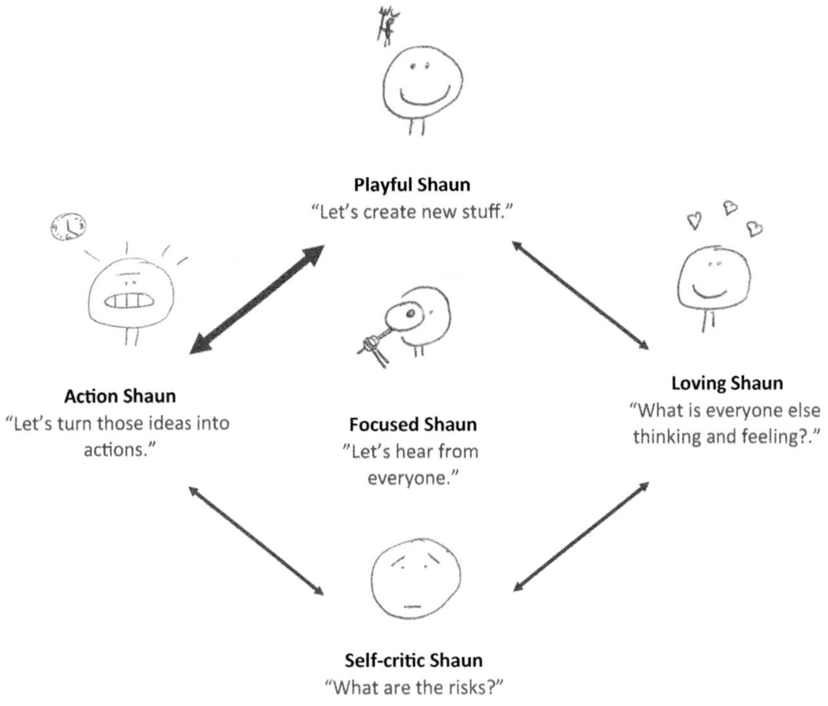

Figure 2.5 The innovation dance.

actions that, upon reflection, were unrealistic. Shaun acknowledged that his career had almost derailed on a couple of occasions because he had driven an innovative new idea too hard, refusing to acknowledge the risk attached to implementation. He requested all his selves to step in when Playful Shaun got excited, to come together in reflection to ensure Playful Shaun's strengths weren't overplayed. Focussed Shaun would facilitate those reflective sessions, and Self-critical Shaun would make sure all risks were acknowledged (Figure 2.5).

Shaun decided to focus on these two scenarios for the time being, believing that progress in these two areas would have the greatest impact on his leadership.

Now that you have had the opportunity to accompany Shaun on his multiplicity journey, we invite you to consider this question. What might be different for you as a leader if you consciously acknowledged that you are not one, but many?

Designing interventions

In Part Two we have outlined a different way of thinking about selves-awareness. We have argued that a multiple perspective on self enables a deeper, more profound exploration of self, helping people to better understand why they show up differently in different scenarios, and to prepare for those scenarios with more purpose and confidence. This capacity to flex effectively in the moment is sorely needed right now as we attempt to navigate the complexity of the world today. The start-point for the OD practitioner in all of this is to ask yourself a question:

1 Where do I stand on the nature of self?

Indeed, you might expand this question to ask yourself, where do I stand on the nature of leadership? In some organizations there is someone who spends time exploring the vast multitude of leadership offerings, deciding which have substance and which have less substance. Sometimes it may not be obvious which offerings have substance, either because the provider is unable to talk confidently about the ideas and theories underlying their programs, or because they support their assertions by citing authors without describing an in-depth understanding of those authors' works. In some organizations, there is no such person. The risk in such organizations is that the leadership offerings chosen have little impact, that they are a waste of money, and/or that multiple offerings are presented offering authoritative yet contradictory advice. We suggest then, that if you are responsible for your organization's leadership offerings, and your strategy is to use outside parties, challenge their assertions and have your own perspective on all things leadership, including the nature of self. That may mean doing your own independent research into the available materials on self (and leadership) to come up with a view you feel confident in holding.

2 *Float* the idea of multiplicity

We are not suggesting you adopt a strict binary position on the nature of self. The evidence around the nature of self is not conclusive. We suggest you seek to become a knowledgeable voice rather than an authoritative voice. Returning to some of the messages we shared on commitment to learning, you may see your task as creating the space for leaders to make sense of available materials for themselves in service of further developing their own practical judgment. So, you may choose to present different perspectives on leadership and self and provide space for people to make sense of these topics for themselves. And if people complain that some of your leadership offerings seem contradictory, you can respond that whilst all your offering are based on robust ideas and theory, they may be different. It is not for you to tell others how to lead. It is for you to share perspectives and co-create opportunities for people to reflect, make sense, and learn for themselves.

3 Strategic deployment of resource

Providers, be they providers of leadership development programs, psychometric tools, coaching services, and so on, all have their own philosophies of self – implicit or explicit. To what extent does their thinking align with your thinking, and to what extent do your providers see their role as being to educate and inform, vs. co-creating a space for personal reflection and learning?

Consider 360° feedback systems for example. These instruments are used just about everywhere nowadays and yet their use may, in many cases, be ineffective or even detrimental to leadership performance. One study reported a decline in performance following feedback in over one-third of cases[28], a highly inconvenient truth considering how ubiquitous the use of 360° instruments has become. Most contemporary approaches to 360° feedback are based on unitary theories of self. That is not to say the use of such tools cannot be helpful. From a multiplicity perspective, the use of these tools is likely to be enhanced if we:

- **Let go of our obsession with numbers.** There is a school of thought that recognises the subjectivity of rater ratings yet seems to think if we collate a whole lot of subjective data we somehow end up with objective data. We don't – what we end up with is a whole lot of subjective ratings rolled up into one meaningless set of numbers. If people are to understand how other people experience them, then they need to understand how they are experienced by different people in different contexts.
- **Dig deep.** Online tools are most popular because they are simple to administer, low cost, and provide us with an alluringly simple depiction of individual leader behaviour. These tools don't, however, provide us with many clues as to how we should make sense of the data. The good tools do provide verbatim comments, but these are often short, written quickly, and without a great deal of thought, by busy people. A much better process is to ask a coach or consultant to go and talk to half a dozen or so key

stakeholders and interview them. Dig out some thoughtful, well-considered perspectives, and draw out from those interviews key themes.

- **Explore contexts.** Good online tools provide separate rater perspectives by audience, for example, line managers, peers, and direct reports. This is useful and may provide some clues as to how people are experienced in different scenarios, in different roles. But this analysis doesn't provide the whole story. Not all raters in one category think the same way or experience the same version of the ratee, and in some of the situations in which a leader operates, some of the roles the leader plays, they are experienced by multiple audiences at the same time.

To illustrate the last two points, we recently conducted a small study, interviewing multiple raters and asking them to describe how they experienced the same ratee in different contexts[29]. Each of the raters we spoke to named multiple contexts in which they experienced the ratee and described quite different versions of that person in each of those contexts. We presented the data back to the ratee, without mentioning multiplicity theory. The ratee *spontaneously* identified five selves in the conversation. He began characterizing those selves and thinking about what triggered each to show up in specific scenarios.

If you do use 360° feedback systems, beware the simple linear thinking that underlies much of the advice we hear as to how we should best use these tools. Use coaches with a more 'constructivist' mindset[30], who see their role as helping the ratee make sense of the data, to get curious as to how the ratee is experienced in multiple contexts, rather than act as a voice of authority as to what the data is telling us about our unitary, 'authentic', self.

4 Guide the reflective process

In Part One we spoke about reflective positivity, the importance of being purposeful in reflection, and other aspects of how to reflect effectively. We suggested that one reason wise leaders reflect is to learn more about self. The content of this section provides further clues as to how leaders might most usefully reflect. The six-step process isn't intended to be linear. Each step contributes to the value of the self-reflective process. Some steps may appeal more to some leaders and other steps to other leaders. The six-step process in its entirety is a big exercise. It constitutes a long-term exploratory agenda. You might choose to tailor your approach to the needs of particular leader populations, presenting simpler frameworks for those audiences seeking a gentler entry point to what is, after all, a lifelong process. Whatever approach you come up with, you can add enormous value to the process by positioning it as an ongoing task, best timed when reflecting on a specific event or series of events, rather than as a discrete almost academic exercise to be conducted in isolation. It's one thing to take some quiet time, on holiday, for example, to reflect on who we think we are as leaders. It's quite another thing to reflect on who we are as a leader in the midst of a difficult conversation, or challenging team meeting, or when something goes particularly well or badly.

5 Leverage group coaching

In the introduction and in Part One we talked about the value of co-reflection, of leaders reflecting together. We outlined at a high level the value and process of group coaching. Inviting people to explore selves together is a powerful process.

Remember *Step Four – test your hypotheses.* If the group coach succeeds in co-creating a psychologically safe space, then willing participants have the opportunity to share their selves perception and get feedback from others in the group – does the individual's hypothesis align with other's experience of the person in-the-moment?

A group coach who understands multiplicity theory and is an advocate of the idea of multiple selves can invite people to consider which selves are showing up in group, and the extent to which those selves are contributing to the success of the group. Remember *Step Five – reflect on inner tension.* Participants may feel torn in the group, in-the-moment, as to how they should show up – to what extent should they be vulnerable and share? To what extent should they lean in and ask questions of others? To what extent are they feeling a compulsion to judge, advise or make suggestions? The coach can encourage people to notice, share and learn from those inner tensions.

If people in the group also work together, then there is a great opportunity for people to support each other in between sessions. If I know how others perceive themselves and I understand which selves they want to bring to different scenarios, then I can offer really useful feedback. I can be a reflective partner in helping others learn from their experiences in the day-to-day.

Group coaching offers a wonderful opportunity for people to learn together, to become more selves-aware together, and to become wiser together. As we said, most willing participants find group coaching to be insightful and supportive, an essential component of an effective learning strategy.

Your 3Ps revisited

Let's look again at the 3Ps (Figure 2.6).

As a leader, what ideas (philosophy) have resonated for you in Part Two? For example, our suggestions that:

- We are multiple
- Authenticity is best defined in terms of how well our different selves know each other and learn to dance with each other
- When we feel torn between two options, it may be different selves pulling us in different directions
- Many of us have at least one or two wise selves
- Better understanding our emotions helps us to become more self-aware

How did our six steps resonate with you in terms of taking steps to become more selves-aware?

As a leadership development professional, how did this section shape your leadership and learning philosophies and what, if anything, will you do differently in the future?

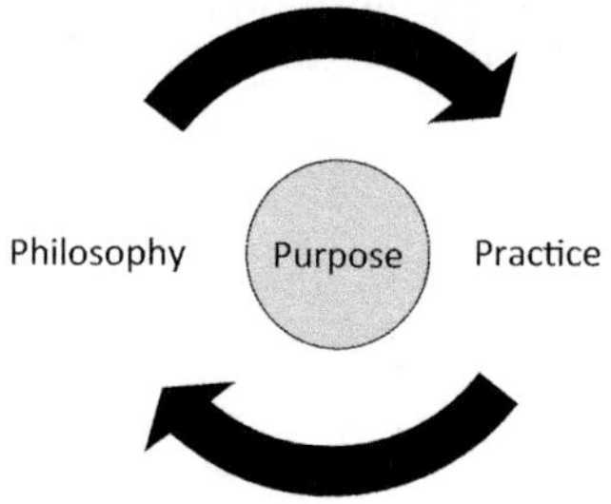

Figure 2.6 The 3Ps.

References

1. For example, Aldwin, C.M., Igarashi, H., & Levenson, M.R. (2019). Wisdom as Self-Transcendence. In: R.J. Sternberg & J. Gluck [Eds.]. *The Cambridge Handbook of Wisdom*. Cambridge; Weststrate, N.M., Bluck, S., & Gluck, J. (2019). Wisdom of the Crowd: Exploring People's Conception of Wisdom. In: R.J. Sternberg & J. Gluck [Eds.]. *The Cambridge Handbook of Wisdom*. Cambridge; and Sternberg, R.J., & Gluck, J. (2019). Wisdom, Morality, and Ethics. In: R.J. Sternberg & J. Gluck [Eds.]. *The Cambridge Handbook of Wisdom*. Cambridge.
2. Wetzel, R. (2015). Who Am I and if so, How Many? Notes on the Myth of Leadership Authenticity. *Journal for Critical Organization Inquiry*, *13(1/2)*, 41–53.
3. Watkins, M. (2003). Dialogue, Development, and Liberation. In: I. Josephs [Ed.] *Dialogicality in Development*. Greenwood.
4. Bachkirova, T. (2022). *Developmental Coaching. Working with the Self.* Open University Press.
5. Weick, K.E. (1995). *Sensemaking in Organizations*. Sage.
6. Edmondson, R. & Woerner, M.H. (2019). Sociocultural Foundations of Wisdom. In: R.J. Sternberg & J. Gluck [Eds.]. *The Cambridge Handbook of Wisdom*. Cambridge.
7. Staudinger, U.M., Lopez, D.F., & Baltes, P.B. (1997). The Psychometric Location of Wisdom-Related Performance: Intelligence, Personality, and More? *Personality and Social Psychology Bulletin*, *23(11)*, 1200–1214.
8. Libet, B., Wright Jr, E.W., & Gleason, C.A. (1983). Preparation- or Intention-to-Act, in Relation to Pre-event Potentials Recorded at the Vertex. *Electroencephalography and Clinical Neurophysiology*, *56(4)*, 367–372.
9. Gazzaniga, M. (1998). The Split Brain Revisited. *Scientific American*, *279(1)*, 50–55.
10. Lester, D. (2010). *A Multiple Self Theory of Personality*. Nova and Rowan, J. (1993) *Discover Your Subpersonalities. Our Inner World and the People in It*. Routledge.
11. Rowan, J. (1990). *Subpersonalities. The People Inside Us*. Routledge.
12. Schwartz, R.C. (1995). *Internal Family Systems Therapy*. Guilford.
13. Carter, R. (2008). *Multiplicity. The New Science of Personality, Identity, and the Self.* Little, Brown, and Company.
14. McConnell, A.R., Shoda, T.M., & Skulborstad, H.M. (2012). The Self as a Collection of Multiple Self-Aspects: Structure, Development, Operation, and Implications. *Social Cognition*, *30(4)*, 380–395.
15. Bachkirova, T. (2022). *Developmental Coaching. Working with the Self.* Open University Press.
16. Gazzaniga, M. (1998). The Split Brain Revisited. *Scientific American*, *279(1)*, 50–55.
17. Berne, E. (1964). *The Games People Play. The Psychology of Human Relationships*. Penguin.
18. Carter, R. (2008). *Multiplicity. The New Science of Personality, Identity, and the Self.* Little, Brown, and Company.
19. Skinner, S. (2015). *Build Your Own Leader Identity. A Practical Guide to Leading Authentically*. Longueville.
20. Schwartz, R.C. (1995). *Internal Family Systems Therapy*. Guilford.

21. Kunzmann, U. & Gluck, J. (2019). Wisdom and Emotion. In: R.J. Sternberg & J. Gluck [Eds.]. *The Cambridge Handbook of Wisdom.* Cambridge.
22. Webster, J.D. (2003). Measuring the Character Strength of Wisdom. *International Journal of Aging & Human Development, 65*, 163–183.
23. Gluck, J., & Bluck, S. (2013). The MORE Life Experience Model: A Theory of the Development of Personal Wisdom. In: M. Ferrari & N. Weststrate [Eds.]. *The Scientific Study of Personal Wisdom.* Springer.
24. Edmondson, R. & Woerner, M.H. (2019). Sociocultural Foundations of Wisdom. In: R.J. Sternberg & J. Gluck [Eds.]. *The Cambridge Handbook of Wisdom.* Cambridge.
25. Gluck, J. (2019). The Development of Wisdom During Adulthood. In: R.J. Sternberg & J. Gluck [Eds.]. *The Cambridge Handbook of Wisdom.* Cambridge.
26. Carter, R. (2008). *Multiplicity. The New Science of Personality, Identity, and the Self.* Little, Brown, and Company.
27. Rowan, J. (1993) *Discover Your Subpersonalities. Our Inner World and the People in it.* Routledge.
28. Kluger, A. N. & DeNisi, A. S. (1996). The Effects of Feedback Interventions on Performance: Historical Review, a Meta-analysis, and a Preliminary Feedback Intervention Theory. *Psychological Bulletin, 119*, 254–284.
29. Lawrence, P. & Bachkirova, T. (2022). A Multiplicity Perspective on 360° Feedback – Challenging Traditional Approaches. *International Journal of Evidence Based Coaching and Mentoring, 21(1)*, 17–30.
30. Maxwell, A. (2017). The Use of Feedback for Development in Coaching. In: T. Bachkirova, G. Spence & D. Drake [Eds.] *The SAGE Handbook of Coaching.* Sage and Maxwell, A. (2020). *Feedback Conversations for Leader Development: An Exploration from Multiple Perspectives.* Unpublished thesis submitted for the degree of Doctor of Philosophy at Oxford Brookes University.

Part Three

Transcend Yourselves

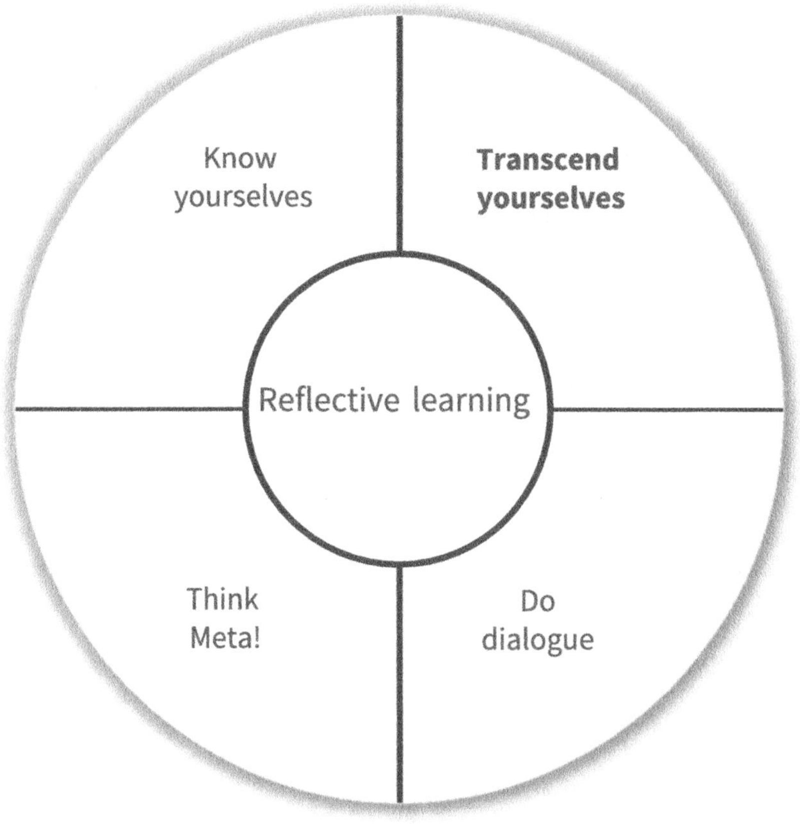

DOI: 10.4324/9781003284826-4

A leadership myth

Leader as Hero

Jean-Francoise arrived at his new organization keen, enthusiastic, and ready to impress. He had achieved great success at his previous company and had been head-hunted for this new role. Before starting the role, he thought about his first 90 days, and how he would ensure he hit the ground running and make the right first impressions with senior management. But his first 30 days, unfortunately, hadn't gone well.

Some of his direct reports clearly didn't appreciate his down-to-earth, no-nonsense style. They seemed reluctant to engage with him outside work and some of them had complained to HR. His peers seemed laid back to the point of being inert. He had approached two of them to co-participate in a new client project. They seemed keen initially but were slow to commit to taking on actions, and slow to complete those actions when they did agree to do something. Jean-Francoise' line manager took him aside one day and explained that people felt he pushed too hard and that they didn't think he was investing enough time in building new relationships. If he didn't change his ways, then he was unlikely to succeed.

Jean-Francoise didn't know what to do. He was behaving no differently from how he had behaved in his previous organization. He had attended leadership programs at the old company, collated lots of feedback, and made every effort to find a style that worked. He was someone who got things done. He was clear and transparent. He issued clear instructions and gave people honest, timely feedback – everything he had been told he should do. So why wasn't it working for him here? He could only conclude that these people weren't results-oriented. They didn't want to work as hard as he did and needed too much 'stroking'. He started to regret having left his previous organization.

Jean-Francoise, like many leaders, has bought into the idea that leadership is about being a great individual, a hero who others look up to for inspiration. It's not surprising that Jean-Francoise has bought into this narrative because many organizations perpetuate it. People are rewarded for their individual efforts. Individuals are held up to others as examples of great leadership. Leaders are expected to be loud, vociferous, and always to the fore.

This narrative misses out on one essential attribute of the wise leader and that is the understanding that we are connected. Wise leaders understand the limits of their own knowledge. They understand that everyone's perspective is subjective and often flawed, and that those perspectives are formed in relationship with others. For Jean-Francoise to be successful in his new organization he may want to spend time reflecting on his past – how he came to be so committed to his current model of leadership? Were he to do so, he would likely realize how many aspects of his current approach to leadership evolved while he was working in his previous organization through conversations with colleagues and leadership development professionals contracted by that organization. This notion of a leader as a great-doer, open, transparent, and clear is not one he developed in isolation. Lots of people helped co-create that notion of leadership. It may or may not build on some of his existing values, shaped earlier in his life, perhaps friends, perhaps close family. To acknowledge this possibility enables Jean-Francoise to elevate his perspective and consider what leadership models might be more useful in successfully transitioning into his new organization. How have those models been co-created and how are they currently co-nurtured by the people working in that organization?

Theory

In Part Two we explored the idea that we are not one, but many. To become more authentic requires getting to know all our various selves and enabling those selves to get to know each other better and to dance together. We become more adaptable, more able to bring our most effective self or selves to any given context. To become more selves-aware helps us to become more impactful, but it only takes us so far. It is one thing to understand our selves, it is another to be able to successfully navigate some of those selves. I may recognize for example, that I am impatient. Just recognizing I am impatient is an important step forward, but it doesn't mean I am always able to manage that impatience or operate independently of the thoughts driving that impatience. This capacity to stand aside from our selves and see ourselves for who we are, and who we are constantly becoming, is what we call selves-transcendence.

The wisdom literature tells us that self-transcendence is important[1]. It tells us that wisdom is about an orientation to the social context[2]. It tells us that wise people can take a self-distanced perspective on complex problems[3]. But not everyone is talking the same language when they talk about self-transcendence[4]. In Part Three we offer you a particular perspective on self-transcendence based on psychological perspectives on leadership.

First, we consider the implications of the co-created self. This idea, that who we are is co-created in relation with others. What consequences does that idea have for how we think about ourselves as leaders? Second, we consider the idea that self-transcendence is developmental, a state attained in the later stages of cognitive development, an aspect of maturity[5]. Third, if we recognize our selves as the manifestations of a co-created process, how does this impact the way we experience others? Fourth, again if we see the emergence of ourselves inextricably bound to the development of others, how is this reflected in our purpose? Finally, before moving to the sections on development, we'll introduce the idea of 'ego-decentering' from the wisdom literature.

1 Co-creation

In Part Two we focused on who we are, advocating a multiplicity approach on the basis that it can enable a deeper, richer level of selves-awareness. But where did these different selves come from? In this section, we reflect on the idea of co-creation. This is the idea that who we are is in a state of constant flux, our selves being subject to an ongoing process of sculpting and change through our relationships and interactions with others.

Let us return to Jean-Francoise, and his first adventures in his new company. If he was more deliberate in his reflections, he might pay attention to some of the narratives flowing through his mind. Those might include beliefs such as:

- Everyone should speak plainly
- Great leaders decide the way forward and inspire others to follow
- I believe in hierarchy and the duty of subordinates to follow their leaders
- Quality is everything
- Work comes first

These beliefs contribute to defining who Jean-Francoise believes himself to be. This sense of self has emerged over the years, fortified by the praise he has always received for the quality of work he produces, by watching authoritative leaders get promoted, by working in environments where people don't go home until everything is done.

A reflective Jean-Francoise decides he needs help. He calls up the leader who originally invited him to apply for the role and asks if she might possibly spare an hour to discuss his predicament over lunch. To his surprise, Karen agrees. Over lunch Karen asks questions to understand his predicament, laying bare some of those narratives that are directing his thinking. By the end of the conversation, Jean-Francoise recognizes that:

- While he speaks plainly, in this organization some people take offence, and he doesn't want to offend people
- He needs to understand his people better if he is to succeed in inspiring them
- He knows how to build relationships and he spent a lot of time in his previous organization getting to know people when he first joined
- His focus on quality is sometimes misplaced
- His relationship with his partner isn't currently in a good place

Jean-Francoise leaves the conversation with a subtly different sense of self. He commits to making more time to get to know people and understand how the organization works. He resolves to make more time to weigh up what's important and what's not. He calls up his wife and asks her out to dinner. As Jean-Francoise heads off home at the end of the day he reflects on how much better he feels. He recognizes his ability to engage and influence others, to delegate to others, to manage multiple demands, and to have the right conversations with the right people. He arrives home a slightly different person to the one who left in the morning. His sense of selves has shifted, through the conversation he had with Karen, but also the conversations he subsequently has with members of his team, his colleagues, and his boss. Jean-Francoise's sense of selves has shifted as a consequence of being faced with a challenge he felt ill-equipped to deal with and as a consequence of engaging in reflective conversation with others. Through that collaborative, co-creative process, a renewed sense of selves emerged. And tomorrow Jean-Francoise will face a new set of challenges, will attempt to address those challenges, and will engage in more conversation with others to make sense of his experience. His sense of selves is again likely to shift and evolve.

2 Self-transcendence as a developmental process

So, we have considered the implications of the co-created self. Now we consider the idea that self-transcendence is developmental. Self-transcendence is a developmental process, according to many of those writing about wisdom[6] and about leadership development. Both pieces of literature draw on theories of adult development, effectively describing different levels of self-transcendence, implying there exist different levels of maturity. There exist many different adult development theories. In this section we consider briefly three different developmental perspectives:

- Robert Kegan's theories of adult development,
- Murray Bowen's ideas around self-differentiation, and
- James Marcia's views on identity.

As you read through this section, think about what you are reading through a multiplicity lens. Much of what you are about to read implicitly assumes we are all singular. But remember Shaun. Shaun identified his Playful Self and described him as being in his twenties. He described his Loving Self as being older, as someone in his forties. Might these different ages correlate to different levels of maturity? Might his different selves be at different levels of development? By further exploring his different selves through the lens of self-transcendence as a developmental process, Shaun will further develop his capacity to stand aside from those selves, to further understand those selves, and to help them work together more effectively.

i Adult development theory

Monica Pasupathi and Ursula Staudinger[7] found that levels of wisdom appear to correlate with levels of moral development as defined by Lawrence

Kohlberg. Kohlberg suggests that we all proceed through at least some of six levels of moral development. Children below the age of 10 or 11 inhabit the first level of moral development in which right and wrong are distinguished by reward and punishment. If I am rewarded for doing something, it must be right. If I am punished, it must be wrong. Moving to the second level, I decide what is right and wrong with reference to what is good for me. I may choose to do something for which I may be punished in the future, because I think that action will serve me well regardless. At the third stage, I care about what others think. If others approve of my action, my action is right. If others disapprove, it is wrong. At the fourth stage, I recognize the value of rules. We need rules because if we didn't have rules then the world would be chaotic. At the fifth stage, we see rules as a social contract, subject to an ongoing process of review and evaluation. At this stage, the rules make sense only if they serve the purpose for which they are intended. At stage six I am guided by universal ethical principles. If I don't believe my society's rules are just, then I will choose not to abide by those rules. Pasupathi and Staudinger found that 38% of the wisest 20% of their sample had reached at least the fifth stage of moral development. Only 15% of the other 80% of their sample had reached stages five or six. This suggests that the more 'developed' we are as adults, the wiser we are likely to be. Kohlberg's theory of moral development is just one of many theories of adult development. All theories of adult development suggest that we all continue to develop beyond our 18th and 21st birthdays, that the way we think continues to evolve and change throughout adulthood.

Robert Kegan is another adult development theorist. We like his theory because it's reasonably straightforward and easy to understand[8]. We cite it here also because it is the developmental theory most often referred to in the leadership literature. We see it show up in lots of leadership development programs, though not always in ways that make lots of sense to participants. People often struggle to translate Kegan's ideas into practice. Kegan describes five stages through which people may progress over the course of their lives. These stages are sequential, he says, and everyone progresses through the stages in the same order, though not everyone proceeds through all five stages. People have labelled Kegan's five stages differently. We are going to use our own language to make it easier to relate his theory to some of the ideas we have already been discussing.

a. *Impulsive*

The impulsive stage is inhabited only by infants and young children. At this stage, we haven't yet succeeded in demarcating ourselves from the world in which we live. When my mum removes the plug from the bath, for example, I may be afraid of being swept down the plughole, struggling to demarcate myself from the rapidly disappearing bathwater.

b. ***Selfish***

This stage is typically inhabited by older children, adolescents, and a few adults. At this stage, we are very aware of our own needs and desires, but less aware of the needs and desires of others. It is not that we *choose* to ignore or neglect others' needs and desires or forget to acknowledge those needs – it is that we are only vaguely aware, if aware at all, that they exist. A person at this stage is likely to come across as thoughtless and self-centred, but to judge them that way may be to hold them to a way of thinking they don't have access to.

c. ***Dependent***

According to the theory, many adults inhabit this stage and never progress beyond. A person at this stage can talk about their values and what's important to them with sincerity and conviction. These values are, however, only partly internalized and may not be wholly coherent. For example, I might tell others how important honesty is to me. My mother talked about the importance of honesty and chastised us when we told lies. My line manager talks about transparency and the importance of delivering the tough message. A partner in the organization talks about practical honesty, the need to tell the truth when directly asked a question. Honesty is important to me because it is important to 'significant others' in my life.

I can speak with great confidence about honesty without being aware that my version of honesty is mostly informed by what other people believe. All is good until I find myself torn between two or more perspectives, all of which are important to me. For example, I notice the client has paid us twice for the assignment we just completed. My line manager says we must let the client know. The partner is equally adamant that we should refund the monies only if the client brings the mistake to our attention. I want to please both my line manager and my partner through the decision I make, but it appears that may be impossible. I get stressed.

d. ***Independent***

At the independent stage, my values and beliefs are more fully internalized. Yes, those values were shaped and continue to be shaped by those around me, but they are my values now. Faced with competing demands from my line manager and the partner, I look inside myself to decide what's right. My internalized value that I call 'honesty' says that we must let the client know they have paid us twice. I still need to navigate the partner's view, because I want to maintain a good relationship with the partner, but I am in no doubt as to what I should do. I am at least reasonably selves-aware and have a good sense of what is important to me and why.

e. *Self-transcendent*

At this stage, I am aware of who I am and what I believe in, and I understand how those beliefs emerged and continue to evolve. I interpret other's behaviours through the same lens. If I find myself in conflict, then I am more likely to frame that conflict in terms of differences in values and beliefs, and I am more likely to respect other values and beliefs. I don't think of the world in terms of there being a single right way of thinking. I recognize that what is important to me is in a constant sense of flux. The differences I experience when engaging with others reflect two sets of values and beliefs, each with their own origins and each with their own journey to come. I recognise how arbitrary my values are, in a sense, in that they would have emerged differently had I led a different life. This stage is sometimes called the 'self-transforming' stage because this constant curiosity in one's own and others' values, and the understanding as to how values and beliefs are formed and continue to evolve, means I am open to my own values and beliefs transforming. We call it the self-transcending stage because it is about being able to see ourselves in relation to others from a distance, and it helps us connect these ideas to the wisdom literature.

Much of the literature on adult development and leadership focuses on the transition from *Dependent* to *Independent*, as does the literature on wisdom. Michael Levenson and colleagues, for example, define self-transcendence in terms of being liberated from external definitions of self[9].

> Brigitte works for a professional services firm and has been invited to apply for partnership. She is both delighted and overwhelmed. She is delighted because she always wanted to be a partner and would love the status and income that go along with being a partner. She would also relish the opportunity to create her own projects and spend more time on the work she finds most worthwhile. She is also overwhelmed. If she applies to be a partner, it means she must go through an extended assessment process that includes building a business case and attending a series of interviews and mock interviews. All of that on top of business-as-usual which is already exhausting. She is reluctant to delegate too much in case the quality of the work declines. Nor does she want to turn down new business opportunities for fear of offending existing partners whose support she needs to succeed. On top of all that she had friends she hasn't seen for a while, who are feeling neglected, a husband and two small children. How will she cope?

We see Brigitte's predicament time and again in the work we do. If we look at her predicament through a developmental lens, we see glimpses of her *Independent* self – the self that wants to be a partner because it will allow her to spend more time on the work she most enjoys. We can also see aspects of her *Dependent* self, the self that values status for status' sake, and that is reluctant to do anything that may tarnish her standing in the eyes of others.

According to the theory, most of us are at the *Dependent* stage, the *Independent* stage, or somewhere in between. For many leaders, their happiness and well-being depend on making a successful transition between the two stages. At the *Dependent* stage, people will often seek assurance from others that they are doing the right thing, particularly if faced with the prospect of upsetting someone, or asked to manage a complex problem. Group norms are important to people at this stage and people are more likely to be perceived as conformists. At the *Independent* stage, people are no longer as sensitive to the wishes of others. They can analyse others' views and make decisions with reference to a set of personal rules and norms that are more integrated and owned. These people are more likely to show up as autonomous, confident, and self-motivated *and* able to discern the needs and norms of others.

Because most people are believed to sit somewhere on a spectrum between *Dependent* and *Independent* many of our leadership offerings are aimed at these people. And so, we see people encouraged to discover their authentic *Independent* self. We see people being encouraged to be braver, to take risks in not pleasing people. We see people being encouraged to think about their values and to consider what it might be like to consistently act in accordance with those values. Most leadership programs target this audience. The design of *The Leadership Circle*, for example, a well-known multi-rater feedback tool, is partly built upon Kegan's third and fourth stages. The Circle has a top half and a bottom half. The more ratings you receive on the top half of the Circle, the more *Independent* you are likely to be. The more ratings you receive on the bottom half of the table, the more *Dependent* you are likely to be. The premise is that the more your ratings lean toward the top half of the Circle versus the bottom half of the Circle, the more effective you are likely to be as a leader.

This is all good but doesn't directly address the question of wisdom. Wisdom requires the individual to move beyond the certainty of *Independence* (stage four) and to embrace *Self-transcendence* (stage five).

> A different version of Brigitte is delighted to be nominated for partnership though she suspects that she will need to shift her thinking if she is to succeed. She has no concerns about the workload. She knows what she wants to achieve, and she knows what she needs to focus on. So long as people think her capable, she will always have more requests for her time than she is able to manage. She focuses on a few specific clients and makes sure she dedicates sufficient time to industry associations and to cultivating a strong team around her. Work does not encroach on weekends, which are for friends and family. This is all good, but she knows also she can become a little too attached to her own way of approaching the world.

Some people annoy her, people she simply doesn't understand, and she can become impatient with those people. To pursue her agenda long term, she knows she will have to build solid relationships with other partners, some of whom think about life quite differently to her. She wonders what she needs to do if she is to be as successful on behalf of the firm as she thinks she can be.

This version of Brigitte sounds like she has reached a stage of *Independence* and is reaching out for *Self-transcendence*. If we want to help leaders to progress beyond independence to self-transcendence, then existing development agendas may not be all that helpful to her. Kegan suggests that only 1% of adults progress toward self-transcendence. If self-transcendence correlates to an extent with wisdom, then that number makes sense to those who believe there are a relatively limited number of wise people in the world. The challenge lies in creating an environment in which more people can become wiser.

We said in the introduction that some organizations understand adult development and have built some of these ideas into their leadership development programs. We also said this isn't often done in a way that enables people to move forward, to access new ways of thinking. Most efforts we've seen present the adult development perspective conceptually. Understanding adult development intellectually doesn't help people access fundamentally different ways of thinking. Later in this section, we'll talk about what you *can* do to enable people to access new ways of thinking.

ii Self-differentiation

We've talked about self-transcendence with reference to a developmental theory. We can also think about self-transcendence and self-differentiation, another set of theories that position our capacity to separate self from others as a developmental process. Murray Bowen designed a Scale of Differentiation[10]. The purpose of the scale is to help us decide for ourselves just how self-differentiated we think we are. We don't include the whole scale here, just a selection of questions. In reading the scale you may be tempted to place your 'self' somewhere on the scale. We encourage you instead to experiment with placing different parts of yourself at different places on the scale (Table 3.1).

Notice there is no 100. Bowen believed that we are all enmeshed, to some extent at least, in some of our relationships. Note also that our degree of self-differentiation does not always correlate to the extent to which we physically distance ourselves from those with whom we feel the tension in the relationship. If I live in the UK and choose to migrate to Australia, that might be because I am highly self-differentiated, or that I am low in self-differentiation and am moving to the other side of the world to put as much distance as possible between myself and the person with whom I have a problematical relationship.

Table 3.1 Murray Bowen's scale of differentiation (simplified)

0–25	Most of life energy goes into loving or being loved Emotionally needy and highly reactive to others. Co-dependent. No boundaries Responses range from automatic compliance to extreme oppositional behaviour
40	Lifelong pursuit of ideal closeness Seeks the approval of others a lot. Preoccupied with creating a good impression Poor emotional skills
60	Acts more on the basis of reason and intellect than simply reacting to feelings Able to think for self rather than simply follow the opinions of others In relationships hesitates to say what he/she thinks. Can hide true thoughts/feelings/needs
75	Can be calm in troubled times Moves between emotional closeness and independent goals Less emotionally reactive but if triggered recovers quickly
85–95	Not likely to be emotionally reactive Capable of listening to the viewpoints of others with an open mind Not overly responsible for others

In considering the extent to which we don't feel self-differentiated we can ask ourselves:

- With whom do I feel somewhat enmeshed?
- What are the behaviours I adopt in order to manage the tension in that relationship?

By reflecting on our selves in this way we may come to better understand different aspects of our selves and further develop the ability to manage those aspects of our selves.

iii Identity theory

There is a whole, separate, literature around the development of identity. Our identity is the story we tell ourselves about who we are. James Marcia described our relationship with identity in terms of exploration and commitment[11]. Exploration is the extent to which we actively pursue a sense of personal identity. Commitment is the extent to which we remain true to that identity. If you position those two dimensions in a simple matrix, then you have four identity statuses (Figure 3.1). Marcia suggests we move through these four statuses as we age and have different life experiences.

If we don't spend much time thinking about our identity and don't behave in a way that appears to connect with any given identity, then we are in a state of *uncertainty*. We have no clear story about who we are, nor are we actively

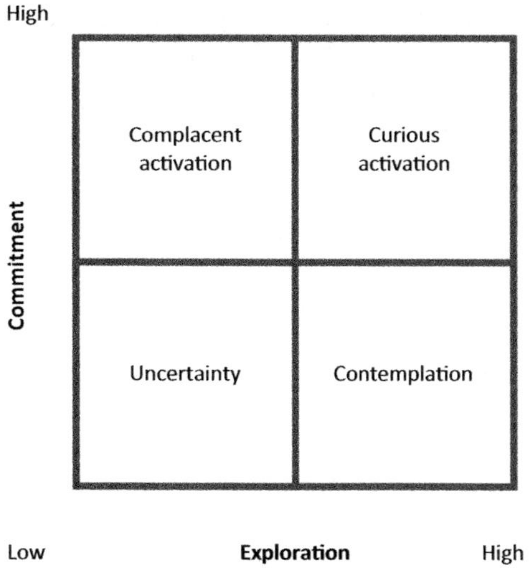

Figure 3.1 Four identity structures.

seeking to gain further insight. We have no strong reference point to refer to in deciding what is the right way to behave. Because we feel so uncertain as to our identity, then we are likely to succumb to the will of others, people who appear to have a stronger sense of identity.

We might move on from uncertainty in one or two different directions. If I am actively curious about exploring my identity further, but not yet committed to behaving in accordance with the identity I am exploring, then I am in a state of *contemplation*. I am interested in my identity but am not active with reference to that identity. Or I may feel a strong sense of identity, an identity I perhaps arrived upon a while ago. I have no interest in further exploring that identity – I am confident in my thinking. We call this a state of *complacent activation*. My identity is fully formed and robust and I have utter certainty in its validity. The wisest, most fully formed, strategy involves both exploration and commitment. I am committed to both further developing my identity and behaving in a way consistent with that identity. This is the state of *curious activation*.

We see these various identity states show up in our work on leader identity. In our global leader identity programs, we help participants move from states of *uncertainty*, in which they are unsure of their leader identity, to *contemplation*, helping them become more willing to notice and name their leadership self. Participants often show up very *uncertain* about their leader identity, an uncertainty that is often accompanied by low levels of self-belief in their capacity to lead. This connection between leader identity, leader self-efficacy, and performance is becoming more recognized[12]. Some of our most meaningful moments working with identity have been witnessing the growth in self-belief that comes with greater clarity of leader-self. Becoming clearer as to my leader identity helps me to believe in myself more as leader, which helps me to become more confident as a leader, and more confident in further exploring my leader self or selves.

Let us now bring this framework to life with reference to Shaun at work. Shaun reports to Henri. Henri has been studying the terms of a joint venture that their company is a part of. The terms of the deal are up for renewal in six months and Henri has spotted a few clauses, buried deep in the agreement, that appear to allow their company to acquire the other company's shares for a relative pittance. Henri is excited and believes that exercising the exit clause is a no-brainer. They have a responsibility to their shareholders to extract maximum value from the contracted relationship. Shaun is much less certain. Exercising the clause will outrage their partner, destroy any prospect of working with them again, and damage their reputation in the marketplace. What Shaun does next reflects his identity status. Table 3.2 details some of the ways Shaun might respond with reference to the identity status framework.

Reflecting on Shaun's experience and on your own selves, where would you place yourselves on this grid?

- Which of your selves would you map to *Uncertainty*?
- Which would you map to *Contemplation*?
- Which are in a state of *Curious activation*?

Marcia tells us that people's progression through these stages is not often linear, with many people oscillating between *Contemplation* and *Curious activation*. What both these states have in common is that the individual remains committed to exploring his or her identity, and to taking time out to consider the implications of different identities before committing to a new set of behaviours. Michael Berzonsky built on this model, suggesting that we all pursue one of three identity styles[13]:

1. ***Self-motivated explorers*** – proactively pursuing an ever-stronger sense of identity, possibly spending time in both *contemplation* and *curious activation*.
2. ***The normative style*** – a fixed approach to an identity that the individual resolutely defends in the face of challenge. This static style is most likely to align with others' viewpoints. This is a version of *complacent activation*.
3. ***The procrastinator*** – letting the situation define what they should do. This might be an exploratory perspective stuck in *contemplation*, or else *uncertainty*.

The wise leader is a self-motivated explorer. Which of your selves is a self-motivated explorer?

Table 3.2 Shaun's identity structures

High	**Complacent activation** Shaun is sure that Henri is wrong. He confronts Henri. As predicted, Henri is annoyed to hear what Shaun thinks and dismisses his views as being naïve and uncommercial. He questions Shaun's readiness to make hard decisions and moves him off the team. Shaun is outraged and sends an e-mail to the CEO.	**Curious activation** Shaun raises his concerns with Henri and asks lots of questions to further understand his views. Leaving the conversation, Shaun still has concerns. He talks to the Board, giving Henri due warning. Henri is furious, but Shaun goes ahead, and the Board put the brakes on Henri's plan. Shaun recognizes his career prospects may have been damaged, but knows he had to act on his values and is satisfied he engaged respectfully with Henri at all times.
Commitment	**Uncertainty** Shaun doesn't feel confident about challenging Henri. He knows Henri would be angry, would question his judgment, and possibly harm his career prospects. Would it be so wrong to exercise the clause? Is it not true that their partner company is ultimately responsible for not having done due diligence on the original contract at the time of signing? Shaun says nothing.	**Contemplation** Shaun senses that what Henri wants to do is morally wrong. Part of him wants to stand up and challenge Henri, but another part of him recognizes he isn't as experienced as Henri. He decides anyway to take advice from people in the industry who he trusts. He isn't ready to let go of a growing conviction that something is wrong and he wants to understand just how robust the voices advising him to take action are.
Low	**Exploration**	High

3 Self-transcendence and respect for others

We have considered the implications of the co-created self, and the idea that self-transcendence is developmental. If we recognize our selves as the manifestations of a co-created process, how does this impact the way we experience others? It is one thing to understand one's selves. It is another thing to allow space for the validity of other people's perspectives. If I have outstanding selves-awareness accompanied by a belief that everyone else should share my beliefs and values, then my capacity to engage effectively with others will be compromised. If I have achieved a degree of self-transcendence, then I will reflect on my selves and the selves of others in ways that help me grow.

The extent to which I achieve self-transcendence relates to the extent I am likely to respect other people's perspectives. Self-transcendence enables me to distance myself from my selves, to see my selves interacting with other's selves, and to be curious about other people's selves, to understand who they are and how they came to be. To self-transcend, our selves require that we:

- Are curious to understand ourselves and our origins better
- Are curious to understand other's selves and origins better
- Are curious to notice ourselves in interaction with others through a lens of values and beliefs, and to better understand those interactions through that lens

The curious mindset pushes us to beckon forth and seek to understand, rather than put up barriers and push away. This capacity to remain curious is what we mean by respect. To respect someone is to be curious about who that person might be and to entertain the possibility that no matter how different that person may appear to be to me, that their perspective is worth my attention and interest. Wise leaders are consistently respectful of others. In 1906 Evelyn Beatrice Hall wrote '*I disapprove of what you say, but I will defend to the death your right to say it*'[14], to illustrate the beliefs of 18th-century philosopher, Voltaire. This is to advocate freedom of speech. To what extent do we, as leaders every day, genuinely encourage others to share what they're thinking?

4 Self-transcendence and purpose

We have considered the implications of the co-created self, and the idea that self-transcendence is developmental, and how such a perspective might impact the way we experience others. If we see the emergence of ourselves inextricably bound to the development of others, how is this reflected in our purpose?

Adult development theorists, such as Kegan, suggest that cognitive development is not a conscious process, it is an unconscious process that kicks in when our current ways of thinking are not servicing us well[15]. Abraham

Maslow suggested that self-actualization cannot be achieved as a pursuit in itself, it is a by-product of a broader pursuit for self-transcendence[16]. Many believe that self-transcendence cannot be a purpose in itself, it is more a consequence of other goal-related activities[17]. All of which is bad news for leaders wanting to go to a workshop to become more self-transcendent and leadership development professionals wanting to oblige them. It does, however, frame the importance of being purposeful. Wise leaders, we are told, are guided not by short-term goals, but by a higher-order purpose[18]. So what is your purpose, as a leader?

The wisdom literature also has something to say about the nature of that purpose. The wise person thinks beyond self-interest and is invested in the well-being of others[19]. Balance theory views wisdom as the successful navigation of self-interest and the interests of others[20]. This is not necessarily a moral standpoint. Wise leaders know that they need to align their interests with the interests of others because no group operates in a vacuum. They understand that we don't succeed without paying attention to the needs of all[21]. People at the self-transcendent stage have a good awareness of how their own and others' values and beliefs are formed. They intuitively understand that their own evolution as an individual is a function of how everyone develops. I know I am not an island. I am not a lone hero. I know that just how others play a part in my development, I influence how others make sense of the world. This is one way to frame that aspect of wisdom that feels most mysterious and elusive, the idea that wise people think and act in service of the collective good.

This lens on collective vs individual motivation implies that this route to being motivated by a common good cannot be taught in a classroom. Those who work in service of their own needs understand intellectually the principle of the collective good, but it isn't how they think or behave. It doesn't matter what stage of adult development we have reached; we can all understand a principle that says, '*it is better to think about others as well as oneself*', but people find it easier to reason wisely about others' predicaments then they do about their own. Attaining a good personal balance requires more than an intellectual appreciation of the idea. We cannot *teach* self-transcendence, but we can create environments conducive to self-transcendence.

Connecting these ideas back to Part One of this book, you may recall how our research revealed that a collective focus is a core feature of the reflective habits of leaders with strong self-belief. Rather than just intellectually appreciating the benefits of the collective good, these leaders integrate a collective focus into their reflective practice, actively reflecting as much on others as on themselves. Their reflections include a consideration of what others need, what obstacles others might be facing, what strategies might support the growth of others, and so on. They purposefully reflect on the collective achievements of the group (team or organization). Leaders with low self-belief, by contrast, focus more on their individual effort. They are more likely to feel burdened and isolated as leaders[22]. Neglecting the interdependencies inherent in their leadership seems to limit their confidence as leaders and their growth as leaders.

5 Ego-decentering

Finally, let us share a term we came across a few times in the wisdom literature. In that literature we find evidence to suggest that wisdom can be emulated by reducing one's focus on selves[23]. Ego-decentering is a tool that invites people to reflect on an issue from an observer's perspective. Or simply to talk about ourselves as a third party. Self-distancing works by lowering emotionality[24].

In Part One we talked about a commitment to reflective learning. In Part Two we talked about applying that commitment to learning more about our selves. In Part Three we have talked about developing our capacity to more deeply understand our selves so that we may transcend those selves to attain a sense of connectedness that serves us well in our efforts to make wiser decisions. In Part Four we will apply this notion of self-transcendence to the specific context in which leaders operate. The role of a leader, above all else, is to effect change. How do wise leaders think about change?

Epilogue

Jean-Francoise Adapts

Jean-Francoise arrived at his new organization keen, enthusiastic, and ready to impress. He had achieved great success at his previous company and had been head-hunted for this new role. Before starting the role, he thought about his first 90 days, and how he would go about building the right relationships with people in the organization.

He spent his first few days just talking to people. He shared his understanding of his role and what he was being asked to achieve but was careful not to go into too much detail. He didn't know to what extent those who hired him had shared their aspirations for the role more broadly in the organization. Initially, he focused more on listening than voicing what he thought he was there to achieve. In just a few days he started to understand who talked to who, and who had what interest in him succeeding.

He also got a sense of how people worked together in the new company. Compared to his old company people paid more attention to how each other were feeling and what might be going on in their personal lives that might impact their presence at work. Jean-Francoise thought back to his last successful project at his old company. They won a massive contract, against the odds, because everyone worked around the clock, and everyone gave each other candid feedback in the moment. Everyone behaved this way, and he was held up as a great role model because he epitomized those behaviours. He wasn't sure that way of behaving would work here. People were more boundaried around their personal lives and held each other to account in leaving work at a reasonable hour and taking accrued leave. People sought permission to give each other feedback, and generally did so in informal surroundings, at lunch or after work.

Jean-Francoise thought back to earlier in his career. It had taken him some time to adjust to his old organization. It took him time to learn how to give effective feedback in the moment. It took him a while to decide if he wanted to work such long hours when the business was busy. He had become more comfortable with that way of working the more time he spent with his old colleagues. There was a mantra in that company, something around getting the job done at all costs. He recognized how much he had enjoyed the adrenalin rush. But it hadn't always been fun. There were times when he didn't get to see his family as often as he liked. At those times he felt torn, taking solace in the fact that his colleagues also told stories about unhappy families. You just worked hard to make it up when the rush was over, was the message. He felt somewhat uncomfortable now, recognizing that he had never sat down and talked about those demands properly with his partner. He had allowed himself to get carried away by the energy at work and hadn't fully questioned some of the assumptions he felt himself surrounded by.

At the same time, Jean-Francoise had enjoyed the pace and the energy. Many people at this new organization were lower energy, more reserved. They didn't all respond with like energy to his enthusiasm. He deliberately slowed down and explored what it was like to engage with their ways of working. They were more thoughtful, more cautious perhaps in their decision-making. The company had gone through a difficult time two or three years ago, with some bad decisions being made. The organization still seemed to be processing those failures. At meetings, people were careful to ensure that everyone was listened to. Meetings took longer than he was used to, but so long as was able to supress his natural energies, he appreciated the depth of conversation people were committed to.

Jean-Francoise didn't know to what extent he would enjoy this way of working in the long term, but he looked forward to exploring it further, and to see to what extent the organization was prepared to accept him, were he to allow some of his energy to surface more often. He was open to his own view of leadership evolving and knew that he would inevitably have an influence on those he worked with. He would make sure it was a positive influence and he committed to experimenting with different approaches to leading forward his piece of work.

After 30 days Jean-Francoise initiated a conversation with his line manager and sought feedback on his first month, both direct feedback and whatever third-party feedback his manager felt comfortable sharing. She told him that people were pleasantly surprised. Based on the people they all knew at his old company they had expected more aggression. They appreciated the efforts he was making to build relationships and to understand how the company worked. She said she felt he seemed to be treading a careful line between the way things currently were, and the way things probably needed to be if the company were to be successful in the long term.

Self-development

To self-transcend our selves is to see our selves for who we are, to understand when and how those selves may have emerged, and to appreciate their contributions. To self-transcend is to engage others as multiple too, and to be curious as to how those selves have emerged and continue to evolve. To self-transcend is to recognize self-transcendence as a cognitive process and to understand how that process might be further facilitated. And to be self-transcendent is to be purposeful, to have an ultimate purpose in our lives that we are committed to achieving.

1 Further explore co-creation

In Part Two we outlined a six-step process for exploring multiplicity of self.

1 List the different roles you play in life
2 Characterise 'you' in each of those roles
3 Identify how many different selves are present across those roles
4 Test your hypotheses
5 Reflect on any tensions between these selves
6 Learn to dance

So far, so good. We have succeeded in further understanding our selves, which enables us to engage more effectively with those selves in service of becoming agile and responsive to all the different situations we come across in life. But we haven't yet fully succeeded in being able to stand aside from those selves such that we can play a more purposeful role in their ongoing development. It is like trying to build a better relationship with another person. If I don't know that person well, I may get annoyed and frustrated when they continually refuse to embark on any new project that requires taking a risk. I avoid talking to them at work and complain about them to others. I may relate to them entirely differently if I have some insight into their lives and understand some of the difficulties they are currently seeking to navigate in their life.

This brings us to another level of introspection, one that you may or may not want to explore. We don't ask you to engage with this work unless you feel entirely comfortable to do so. We invite you to decide for yourself how useful (or not) you believe it will be to dig deeper into your origins of selves. In seeking to further understand your origins of selves we invite you to consider who may have played a significant role in co-creating each of your selves. We suggest three possible sources of influence.

i Parents

As we said, this stage is entirely optional, of course. If you are aware of any trauma in your childhood, or your relationship with either of your parents was traumatic, then we suggest you skip this stage or embark upon it with the support of someone. If you *are* happy to explore those relationships, then read on.

In wondering to what extent he felt self-differentiated, Shaun considered Action Shaun. The scale talked about 'extreme oppositional behaviour' as an index of low self-differentiation. He didn't think Action Shaun demonstrated *extreme* oppositional behaviour, but he was oppositional. Shaun recognized how that aspect of himself may have emerged as a protective mechanism in early relationship with his father. In wondering how to explore that relationship further Shaun found something called 'the script questionnaire'. The script questionnaire was created thirty years ago by two psychotherapists, Maggie and Jeff White[25]. They came up with a simple methodology for beginning to understand the impact of mum and dad on the way we look at life. The questionnaire comprises ten questions you can try answering for yourself. Shaun answered the questions as follows:

1 Imagine you are sitting across from your mum, and imagine her saying to you "I am most happy with you when …	*… you are calm and considerate and friendly to everyone.*
2 Imagine you are sitting across from your dad, and imagine him saying to you "I am most happy with you when …	*… you do as you are told. When you make sensible and conservative decisions, not taking any risks.*
3 When you were little, what was it about you that most upset your mum – or that she was afraid of in you?	*Anger.*
4 When your mother lets you know she does not like you being like this, what do you feel?	*Resigned/isolated.*

5	What do you do when you feel like this?	*Withdraw.*
6	When you were little, what was it about you that most upset your dad – or that he was afraid of in you?	*Anger/not listening to him.*
7	When your father lets you know she does not like you being like this, what do you feel?	*Frustrated/annoyed.*
8	What do you do when you feel like this?	*Lose my temper.*
9	Think of a sentence (or phrase) to describe the theme of your mum's life.	*Try your best and be polite to others.*
10	Think of a sentence (or phrase) to describe the theme of your dad's life.	*Work hard. Always achieve. Take no risks.*

Once you've answered all the questions then consider your answers in terms of:

(1) and (2) The way you should be successful in life
(3) and (6) The way you should not be
(4) and (7) Your unhappy feeling responses
(5) and (8) The decisions you made to cope with stress
(9) and (10) The models of 'how to live life' you learned from your parents

Shaun reflects on his answers and writes:

(1) (2) You should be calm, considerate, obedient and risk averse
(2) (6) You should not get angry or disobey
(3) (7) If unhappy, you feel resigned, isolated, frustrated, and annoyed
(4) (8) To cope with stress, you withdraw and lose your temper
(9) (10) Models to live life by are to work hard, take no risks, and be polite to everyone

In reviewing his answers, Shaun went back to his hypothetical selves. He saw the desire to be always calm in Focussed Shaun especially, and he saw Focussed Shaun as a place he went to when feeling threatened by others' anger, or in the face of others feeling intimidated by others. He saw how Action Shaun may have emerged to protect him from being overwhelmed by his father's need to control and dominate. He recognized also how much time he spent alone as a child, how he always chose to withdraw from some of his parent's behaviours rather than stay in close proximity and get angry. He recognized how Self-critical Shaun, now very quiet, had been much more active in his childhood and early adulthood, rendering him unable to manage a constructive relationship with his father. Shaun revisits his five work selves and adds a few notes (Table 3.3).

Table 3.3 Shaun's five work selves revisited

Self	*Behaviours*	*Emotions*	*Drivers*	*Says things like …*
Action Shaun	Focussed Unbending Impatient *Directive*	Determination Focus Impatient *Anger*	Achieve	"Let's do it."
Playful Shaun	Spontaneous Playful Intimate Doing it!	Joy Happiness Love Bounce Drive *Freedom*	Have fun Progression Health Vitality	"Let's just try it?"
Loving Shaun	Attentive Loving Sociable Engaging Supportive	Love Compassion Empathy Determination Respect Happiness	Support Nurture Collaboration	"How are you feeling?"
Focussed Shaun	Thinking Serene	Calm Thoughtful Intentional Quiet *Grateful*	Learn	"What's going on here?"
Self-critical Shaun	Attentive Compliant	Connection Self-doubt Anxiety	Harmony	To self: "What are you doing wrong?"

In this case, Shaun's reflections on his childhood have enabled him to refine his analysis. In other cases, people may discover whole new selves that don't emerge in the role analysis.

ii Specific others

John Rowan suggests we sometimes create new selves to help us manage difficult situations[26]. For example, if I feel frequently intimidated by others, I might call upon an inner Hulk, or another fictional character, to help me manage more ably.

Shaun thought about a time in his career when the decision was made to sell the business he was leading. The decision to sell was deeply upsetting for many employees, partly because they didn't want to lose their jobs, partly because they enjoyed working with the people they worked with, and partly because they had been highly committed to the success of the business. It was going to take up to 12 months to sell the business, and Shaun realized that everyone would be watching him very carefully every minute of every day, to gauge his mood, to watch him from afar in conversation, all to pick up on any signs as to whether the sale was going well or not. If the sale went well, then people hoped that most of them would retain their positions and that the new owner would be supportive and good to work for.

Shaun felt sad and tired. So, he thought of a leader he had worked for in a previous role – Jeff. Jeff was always bright, energized, and determined. Nothing phased him. He strode into work every day with a cheerful, determined look on his face and dealt with every challenge with great resolve. Shaun recalled how he had started walking into work like Jeff had walked into work. How he had purposefully maintained a bright positive attitude even when he felt tired and under pressure. That aspect of himself had shades of Focussed Shaun but was more outgoing and engaging. He added an internalized 'Jeff' to his list. Jeff was determined, energetic, and thoughtful, liable to sudden outbursts of emotion. He was direct, cheerful, and no-nonsense. His drivers were to support others in doing their best in service of achieving a specific outcome. He said things like '*What's going on with you?*' and '*What's the issue?*' and '*Keep going!*'. Like Action Shaun, he was male and in his forties, but he was a large man, physically strong. He was a bit like Action Shaun, but not impatient nor directive, indeed his whole focus was on enabling others to take risks and to learn from their mistakes.

iii Our prevailing culture

Sometimes it's hard to pin down exactly who may have influenced the evolution of our different selves. We learn some of our behaviours from a multitude of others. That includes parents and friends and everyone else. It includes some of the norms of the cultures in which we are raised. Those norms are not all directly expressed to us, nor are we necessarily aware of their influence. Those norms may include messages we read in the papers, watch on television, see in films. Of course, if we are not aware of their influence then we can only hypothesize how they may have influenced us in becoming the people we are, but hypotheses are good, and we can test hypotheses.

Shaun reflected on his childhood growing up in countryside England. He reflected on his early adulthood at a university in the north of England and completing a PhD in London. He reflected on spending time living and working in Australia, Spain, Portugal, and Japan, and his most recent years bringing up a family in Australia. He speculated on how culture may have shaped the person he was. He thought about some of those contexts and started to write up a list of possible cultural norms that may have shaped the growth of some of his selves:

- **Be self-sufficient**, a value he learned as a small child, feeling he was supposed to be able to deal with day-to-day challenges himself and not require emotional support from parents or teachers.
- **Care for others**, a value that emerged strongly for him when living in the north-east of England at a time when the government of the day was closing down whole industries without making provision for those impacted.

- **Men provide for their families,** a consequence of growing up at a time when most mothers stayed at home to look after the house and raise children. TV shows and films showed men doing the work and women doing the housework and raising children.
- **Bosses rule.** He recalled his first visits to potential employers in the late eighties. He was introduced to senior leaders who were openly bossy with their subordinates while he and other potential recruits were watching. He remembered his own father coming home miserable and unhappy from work every day. He recalled TV shows and their depictions of authority.

In reflecting on the impact of culture in his own development, he recognized, for example, how Action Shaun was quite boundaried and expected others to manage regardless. Loving Shaun was more empathic and caring and considerate, willing to go out of his way to help others. He recognized the tension between these two selves, and the tensions they experienced with each other when relating to others.

2 Adult development and multiplicity

With reference to adult development theory, we find that the idea we are each located somewhere on a spectrum from one to five, or *Impulsive* to *Self-transcendent* doesn't resonate with many people. It makes sense intellectually but doesn't make sense to people from a personal perspective. Most people recognize that they do think, sometimes at least, through the *Dependent* lens (stage three). Many of us can also cite examples of thinking in different contexts through an *Independent* lens (stage four). As the theory goes, that would place most of us somewhere between *Dependent* and *Independent*. But some people identify with all four stages – Selfish, Dependent, Independent, and Self-transcendent.

Shaun, for example, can maintain a holistic perspective while navigating challenging conversations. People compliment him on his ability to stay calm and respectful (*Self-transcendent*). But in certain scenarios, on certain days, he seems to lose some of that calm. He gets overly excited, overly attached to his own perspective. He speaks with great certainty and is dismissive of others' views (*Independent*). The other day, when asked to present to an audience of 500 people he felt scared, worried he might say something silly or start to stutter (*Dependent*). At the weekend, Shaun's internet stopped working. He rang the helpline and was frustrated at their lack of interest in his predicament. He started shouting down the phone, oblivious to the fact he was talking to another human being (*Selfish*).

In thinking how to apply adult development to theories of a single self it is useful to think of the self as being made up of skins, like an onion[27]. When I am tiny I might have just the one *Impulsive* skin. As I get older, I grow a *Selfish* skin. I am now capable of thinking through either lens. Which lens I think through will depend on the situation. As I enter early adulthood I might grow a *Dependent* skin, finding myself beholden to other's beliefs and views in some contexts. Then I may start growing an *Independent* skin, such that I find myself quite certain about myself in relationship to others – sometimes. This is a useful way of thinking about adult development in that it helps us make sense of how we can access different ways of thinking in different circumstances.

Another way to accommodate this perspective is to refer once more to our multiplicity model. Shaun revisits his five selves. He wonders how each self emerged and the extent to which each has developed. He recognizes how Action Shaun sometimes forgets to pay attention to how others are feeling. He just pushes ahead no-matter-what. Action Shaun is not un-empathetic but believes squarely in the value of taking actions and giving it a go. Playful Shaun gets carried away by his own thoughts and feelings and can appear oblivious to the needs of others too. Is he *Selfish* perhaps? Shaun believes he is most likely *Independent* because he likes to play with others and is good at reading others' thoughts and feelings – like Action Shaun he just tends to forget to check in when engrossed in his own agenda. Loving Shaun is somewhere between *Dependent* and *Independent*. Sometimes he gets pulled into wanting to make others happy, other times he is better at managing boundaries whilst remaining concerned and empathic. Focussed Shaun helps Loving Shaun to maintain those boundaries and helps Self-critical Shaun manage his responses to people who seems dissatisfied with Shaun.

Action Shaun	Independent – pushes ahead with his own agenda
Playful Shaun	Independent – focusses on having fun
Loving Shaun	Dependent/Independent – connects with others
Focussed Shaun	Self-transcendent – able to accommodate multiple perspectives
Self-critical Shaun	Dependent – sounds the alarm when others are displeased

Shaun finds this analysis useful. It reminds him how important it is that he brings forth Loving Shaun and Focussed Shaun when asked to manage complex issues, and how important it is that he carefully manages the contributions of Action Shaun and Playful Shaun in situations where it is important to acknowledge and respect the view of others.

As we said, adult development theorists suggest we cannot consciously learn how to attain a new level of development. The process is a subconscious process that happens when our current ways of thinking don't seem to be working. This perspective is consistent with Michael Levenson's perspective on wisdom, which says stress is a source of self-transcendence[28]. Stress shatters our existing worldview and stirs us to seek a new worldview, one that is more helpful. The *Selfish* way of thinking (stage two) may help us get our own way if we have absolute positional power. But there are few examples of absolute positional power. Most leaders need support from others if they are to succeed, which requires the capacity to understand what others are thinking and feeling, and to seek to satisfy some of those needs and desires. This *Dependent* way of thinking (stage three) serves us well so long as we don't encounter multiple needs and desires coming from different people, all of whom we want to satisfy. At that point, we are likely to struggle unless we develop an internal compass to help come up with independent conclusions as to what we should do next. An *Independent* way of thinking (stage four), which includes the ability to engage effectively with others, will help us steer a path through conflicting perspectives. We likely approach our task with confidence and certainty, a belief in our capacity to discern the right answer to a complex problem. But the *Independent* approach may not serve us so well in a world where we need to understand, not only what people are thinking and feeling, but how they are thinking. If we are to engage effectively with people who think very differently to us, we need to find space for divergence. This requires us to be *Self-transcendent* (stage five).

If I see the world through a *Dependent* lens, and everything is going well, then I am unlikely to seek a different approach to the world. If, however, I am constantly finding myself attacked and criticized by those I respect because every decision I make, makes someone happy and someone else cross, then I will seek another way of approaching the world. I am driven to do so by the anxiety and stress I experience in constantly having to manage discord. I thrive on harmony and am surrounded by conflict. Stress compels us to explore new ways of thinking. So, we should look for opportunities to be stressed?! Yes and no. We don't encourage you to go jump off cliffs (at least not without a parachute), but we do encourage you to purposefully step outside your comfort zone. And remember *symbiotic positivity* – seek out others to accompany you on the journey.

3 Be purposeful

Levenson[29] talks about stress as a route to self-transcendence, and also purpose. This doesn't mean people purposefully seeking to become transcendent. It means people who have a strong purpose in life are more likely to attain self-transcendence. Levenson spoke to nuns, who talked about self-transcendence in terms of i) spending time contemplating and quietening the ego, ii) listening, being open to and respectful of others, and iii) striving to achieve an ultimate purpose. This makes intuitive sense. Self-transcendence is not a wholly cognitive process, but it sounds like an effortful process, a process likely to kick in only if we have some ultimate purpose in mind. Independent Brigitte, for example, seeks new ways of doing things because she has an ultimate purpose in terms of what she wants to achieve at her company. If Brigitte was happy to take a partner role purely for the money and the prestige, it's unlikely she would be so driven.

It's easy to talk about purpose, harder to define for ourselves what our purpose might be. Why do you want to lead, other than for the extra money and status? For some people, money and status are enough, but not for most people. Most of us want our lives to be meaningful and we want to make some greater contribution, but what that contribution might be is often hard to articulate. Part of the problem may be that we feel obliged to articulate our purpose in one short, noble, sentence. But trying to craft such a statement may not be helpful. From a multiplicity perspective trying to define one single purpose may be too hard when we have multiple voices expressing different priorities.

Purpose may be more usefully defined as a *collection* of goals and intentions that give life direction and meaning[30]. If we buy into the idea that we have multiple selves, then it makes sense that our purpose in life is likely to be multilayered. Shaun starts to unpack what his purpose as a leader might be, thinking about purpose through the lens of each of his work selves.

Action Shaun	Be productive
Playful Shaun	Enjoy life and create
Loving Shaun	Connect with others
Focussed Shaun	Grow and develop
Self-critical Shaun	Be careful

Shaun finds this useful. Searching for multiple aspects of purpose is easier than trying to identify one single overarching purpose in life. He starts taking notes about himself as leader. He realizes that what motivates him is the opportunity leadership offers him to help others to:

- Achieve things for themselves
- Think differently
- Connect across communities
- Grow and develop
- Look after their health and wellbeing

According to the wisdom literature, purposeful wise leaders have more 'grit'[31]. Grit is about perseverance. The wise leader is committed to her objectives for the long haul. The wise leader works for an organization only if she can see a way to achieve her purpose within the parameters of that organization. She will need to see alignment between her objectives and the goals of the organization. If she does choose to work with that organization, then that organization can count on her remaining committed to her work for the duration. The wise leader is willing to work hard without immediate satisfaction and enjoyment and is good at working through uncertainty. Amidst uncertainty the wise leader stays focussed on the ultimate objective and remains committed to that objective. Notice how this 'grit' almost inevitably compels this leader to understand herself in relation to others. If this leader goes about her work solely driven by her own needs and desires, then her capacity to influence others remains limited. To be successful she is going to have to learn to read an organization's intent. She must successfully navigate others needs and intentions, even if those needs and intentions are hard to discern. Quite possibly subconsciously, she is inevitably driven to understanding herself better in relation to others. There exists within her a subconscious drive to self-transcend.

How do we go about being more purposeful? Start by asking yourself the following questions:

1 What is your purpose? Remember, your purpose may be multi-layered.
2 How do each of your selves relate to this purpose?
3 Which of your selves may need to work harder to bring your purpose to life?

4 De-centre your ego

As we said, there is evidence to suggest that wisdom can be emulated by reducing one's focus on selves, and this can be achieved by reflecting on issues from an observer perspective, or just by talking about ourselves as a third party. This process is particularly helpful in disentangling us from the emotions we often experience in managing complexity and uncertainty. You can try this on your own, or in talking with others.

In working through the issue by yourself, try a form of journaling. Write about the scenario you are facing and the challenges you are trying to navigate. But write about yourself in the third person, not the first person. What new insights emerge for you? How are you now feeling?

Similarly, if sharing your predicament with others, talk about yourself as he or she. Explain why you are talking about yourself in the third person, to avoid the other person giving you strange looks. Again, what new insights emerge for you? How are you now feeling?

Designing interventions

In Part Two we outlined a different way of thinking about selves-awareness. We argued that a multiple perspective on self enables a deeper, more profound exploration of self, helping people to better understand why they show up differently in different scenarios, and to prepare for those scenarios with more confidence. We invited you, as an OD practitioner, to ask yourself where you stand on the idea of multiplicity, to consider floating the idea of multiplicity with people in your organizations through your offerings, and to work with providers whose views of self you feel comfortable with. We also invited you to consider the six-step process as a guiding framework for developing your own frameworks for specific audiences and learning scenarios.

In Part Three we have suggested that wise leaders have the capacity to self-transcend. This means developing a deeper understanding of selves and the way selves are born and evolve. This understanding presents the leader with more choice as to who they want to be, and intention as to what conversations they wish to engage with as part of the co-creative process. To develop a deeper understanding of selves requires exploring the past as well as the present. If you are to offer leaders the opportunity to explore the past, then there are some important principles you may want to think about.

1 Have a perspective on adult development

We know of various organizations that include adult development theory in their programs in some guise, often Kegan's theories or similar cognitive developmental theories. We know of fewer organizations whose OD professionals have a good understanding of adult development theory themselves and a well-thought-through rationale for the inclusion of those theories in their programs. Many organizations outsource their programs and are philosophically indifferent as to what models and frameworks are included on those programs. We encourage you to educate yourself on these theories before asking someone else to educate your leaders. There are lots of providers out there, each with their favourite theory and/or personal interpretation of that theory and/or belief as to how that theory can be brought to life in a practical sense.

We have come across lots of companies who are very much attached to a particular theory, to a particular version of that theory, and less focused on helping leaders translate those ideas into practice. If we take Kegan theory for example, what is your interpretation of that theory? Do you believe we can plot people at a single locus on a scale of one-to-five? Do you believe people are either dependent or independent or self-transcendent? This is the most common interpretation of Kegan theory and yet it's one (as we said before) we find to be quite disempowering for many people, one they find hard to relate to or make sense of. What is your view? Do you have one? And what guidance do you offer people in terms of gaining access to different levels of development? Many organizations teach the model quite didactically, assuming that teaching the model conceptually enables people to access different ways of thinking. In our view (as have already explained) teaching adult development theory by itself doesn't help people become wiser. What is your view?

2 Contract clearly

In Part One we suggested you *invite – don't coerce*. When it comes to self-transcendence, *invite – don't coerce* becomes an essential principle. Not only in service of you allocating your resources well, but to fulfil your obligations as an employer to provide duty of care. It is not your right as an employer to oblige people to explore their past. You may invite people to embark upon such a journey, but you must ensure that the people you invite believe they have real choice. If, for example, I believe I can decline an offer to participate on your program but believe that to do so will limit my career prospects in your organization, then I am not being offered real choice. You must therefore engage with the leadership of your organization as well as potential participants, if you are to be able to offer people genuine choice, and to contract effectively. By contracting, we mean coming to an agreement. We don't mean that you necessarily must prepare written contracts. Indeed, we would warn you against a process that asks people to commit to an entire program before the program starts and before people have experienced a program. The contracting process needs to be ongoing. People need to be given real choice as to whether they participate in specific exercises, rather than it be assumed people have signed their lives away in agreeing upfront to participate in a program.

3 Engage the right partners

If you plan to invite people to explore origins of selves, then your facilitators, coaches, and other providers must be qualified to work with people in that space. They must understand the importance of contracting, must understand when and how to contract effectively, and must be experienced in holding the space for people. Stories abound of unqualified people inadvertently coercing people to participate in exercises they are unsure about. If you work with groups, then you and your partners need to understand group dynamics and be sensitive to the presence of peer pressure. Your partners don't necessarily need to be therapists or counsellors, but they need to understand the boundaries between the work you are doing and counselling/therapy. They need to understand where it is appropriate to go and where it is not. They need to know how to provide a supportive space and where it is inappropriate to visit regardless of their capacity to offer support.

4 Go l-o-n-g and support reflection

Again, we find ourselves repeating some of the principles from Part One. These principles are essential when it comes to facilitating greater levels of self-transcendence. The theory says that self-transcendence emerges from ongoing exposure to challenge and some degree of stress, as people attempt to navigate degrees of complexity they haven't previously had access to. Self-transcendence is emergent and emerges over time. It isn't a theoretical model that can be taught and left with someone to then go and implement by themselves, yet that is how it is often presented.

A few years ago, program participants were often asked to take on challenging projects in addition to their day jobs. We see that less often, thankfully, as most people these days have challenging enough roles. Rather than seek to create new challenging environments for attendants, we suggest you invite people to attend programs while they are transitioning into new, more challenging roles. It is during these transitions that people are likely to experience overwhelm, when they find that old ways of thinking are no longer serving them well. This again means you ought *invite – not coerce*, because some people do regard leadership development programs as intellectual endeavours, to be embarked upon when I am relatively relaxed and time-rich. From the wisdom perspective a leadership program is an offer to accompany someone on a role transition. Your role then becomes to commit to support the individual over a period of time, to create supporting structures, including opportunities to reflect with others, and to challenge and support people in their efforts to manage higher levels of stress.

Your 3Ps revisited

Let's look again at the 3Ps (Figure 3.2).

As a leader, what ideas (philosophy) have resonated for you in Part Three? For example, our suggestions that:

- We are co-created, and remain in a process of co-creation, through our interactions with others
- Our different selves progress through stages of development, from *selfish* to *self-transcendent*
- That process can be facilitated by making time for reflective learning at times of stress
- Self-transcendence is a by-product of being more generally purposeful
- Our sense of purpose is multi-layered
- Wise leaders have a *collective* sense of purpose

How did our suggestions for self-development resonate with you in terms of taking steps to become more selves-transcendent?

- How useful was it to think more deeply about the origins of your different selves?
- How will you seek out experiences beyond your comfort zone,
- Are you motivated to try some ego-centering?

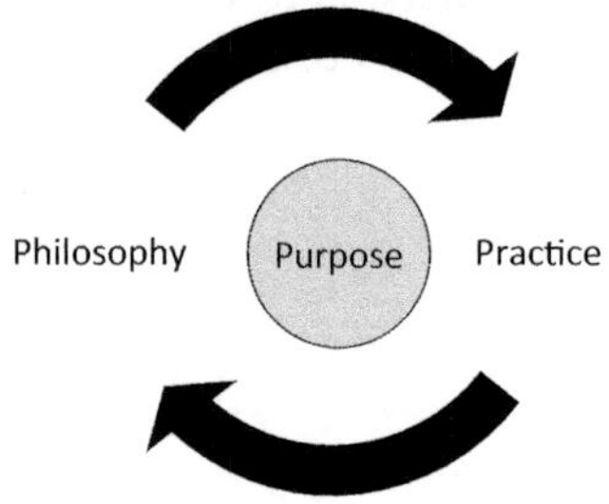

Figure 3.2 The 3Ps.

As a leadership development professional, how did this section shape your leadership and learning philosophies and what, if anything, will you do differently in the future?

References

1. Staudinger, U.M. & Gluck, J. (2011). Psychological Wisdom Research: Commonalities and Differences in a Growing Field. *Annual Review of Psychology*, *62*, 215–241.
2. Baltes, P.B. (2004). Wisdom as Orchestration of Mind and Virtue. *Max Planck Institute for Human Development*.
3. Sternberg, R.J. & Gluck, J. (2019). Wisdom, Morality, and Ethics. In: R.J. Sternberg & J. Gluck [Eds.]. *The Cambridge Handbook of Wisdom*. Cambridge.
4. Aldwin, C.M., Igarashi, H., & Levenson, M.R. (2019). Wisdom as Self-Transcendence. In: R.J. Sternberg & J. Gluck [Eds.]. *The Cambridge Handbook of Wisdom*. Cambridge.
5. Wink, P. & Helson, R. (1997). Practical and Transcendent Wisdom: Their Nature and Some Longitudinal Findings. *Journal of Adult Development*, *4*, 1–15.
6. Reed, P.G. (2001). Toward a Nursing Theory of Self-Transcendence. *Advances in Nursing Science*, *13*, 64–77.
7. Sternberg, R.J. & Gluck, J. (2019). Wisdom, Morality and Ethics. In: R.J. Sternberg & J. Gluck [Eds.]. *The Cambridge Handbook of Wisdom*. Cambridge.
8. Kegan, R. (1998). *In Over Our Heads: The Mental Demands of Modern Life*. Harvard University Press.
9. Levenson, M.R., Jennings, P.A., Aldwin, C.M., & Shiraishi, R.W. (2005). Self-Transcendence: Conceptualisation and Measurement. *International Journal of Aging and Human Development*, *60*, 127–143.
10. Kerr, M. & Bowen, M. (1988). *Family Evaluation: An Approach Based on Bowen Theory*. Norton.
11. Marcia, J.E. (1966). Development and Validation of Ego-identity Status. *Journal of Personality and Social Psychology*, *3*(*5*), 551–558.
12. Steele, A.R. & Day, D.V. (2018). The Role of Self-attention in Leader Development. *Journal of Leadership Studies*, *12*, 17–32.
13. Berzonsky, M.D. (1989). Identity Style: Conceptualization and Measurement. *Journal of Adolescent Research*, *4*(*3*), 268–282.
14. Beatrice Hall, E. (1906). *The Friends of Voltaire*. Good Press.
15. Kegan, R. (1998). *In Over Our Heads. The Mental Demands of Modern Life*. Harvard University Press.
16. Maslow, A.H. (1969). The Farther Reaches of Human Nature. *Journal of Transpersonal Psychology*, *1*, 1–9.
17. Aldwin, C.M., Igarashi, H., & Levenson, M.R. (2019). Wisdom as Self-Transcendence. In: R.J. Sternberg & J. Gluck [Eds.]. *The Cambridge Handbook of Wisdom*. Cambridge.
18. Edmondson, R. & Woerner, M.H. (2019). Sociocultural Foundations of Wisdom. In: R.J. Sternberg & J. Gluck [Eds.]. *The Cambridge Handbook of Wisdom*. Cambridge.
19. For example – Staudinger, U.M. (2019). The Distinction Between Personal and

General Wisdom: How Far Have We Come? In: R.J. Sternberg & J. Gluck [Eds.]. *The Cambridge Handbook of Wisdom*. Cambridge.

20. Sternberg, R.J. (2019). Why People Often Prefer Wise Guys to Guys Who Are Wise: An Augmented Balance Theory of the Production and Reception of Wisdom. In: R.J. Sternberg & J. Gluck [Eds.]. *The Cambridge Handbook of Wisdom*. Cambridge.
21. Sternberg, R.J., & Gluck, J. (2019). Wisdom, Morality and Ethics. In: R.J. Sternberg & J. Gluck [Eds.]. *The Cambridge Handbook of Wisdom*. Cambridge.
22. Skinner, S. (2021). *Understanding the Influences on Leader Self-Efficacy: A Constructivist Grounded Theory Study*. Doctorate thesis. University of Wollongong.
23. Grossman, I. (2017). Wisdom in Context. *Perspectives on Psychological Science, 12(2)*, 233–257.
24. Santos, H.C., Huynh, A.C., & Grossman, I. (2017). Wisdom in a Complex World: A Situated Account of Wise Reasoning and Its Development. *Social and Personality Psychology Compass, 11(10)*.
25. White, M. & White, J. (1986). Scripts and Marathons. *Transactional Analysis Journal, 16(1)*, 47–49.
26. Rowan, J. (1993) *Discover Your Subpersonalities. Our Inner World and the People in it*. Routledge.
27. Lawrence, P. & Moore, A. (2019). *Coaching in Three Dimensions. Meeting the Challenges of a Complex World*. Routledge.
28. Levenson, M.R., Jennings, P.A., Aldwin, C.A., & Shiraishi, R.W. (2005). Self-Transcendence: Conceptualization and Measurement. *International Journal of Aging and Human Development, 60*, 127–143.
29. Levenson, M.R., Jennings, P.A., Aldwin, C.A., & Shiraishi, R.W. (2005). Self-Transcendence: Conceptualization and Measurement. *International Journal of Aging and Human Development, 60*, 127–143.
30. Ryff, C.D. (1989). Happiness Is Everything, or Is It? Explorations on the Meaning of Psychological Wellbeing. *Journal of Personality and Social Psychology, 57(6)*, 1069–1081.
31. Duckworth, A.L. & Gross, J.J. (2014). Self-Control and Grit: Related but Separable Determinants of Success. *Currents Directions in Psychological Science, 23*, 319–332.

Part Four

Think Meta

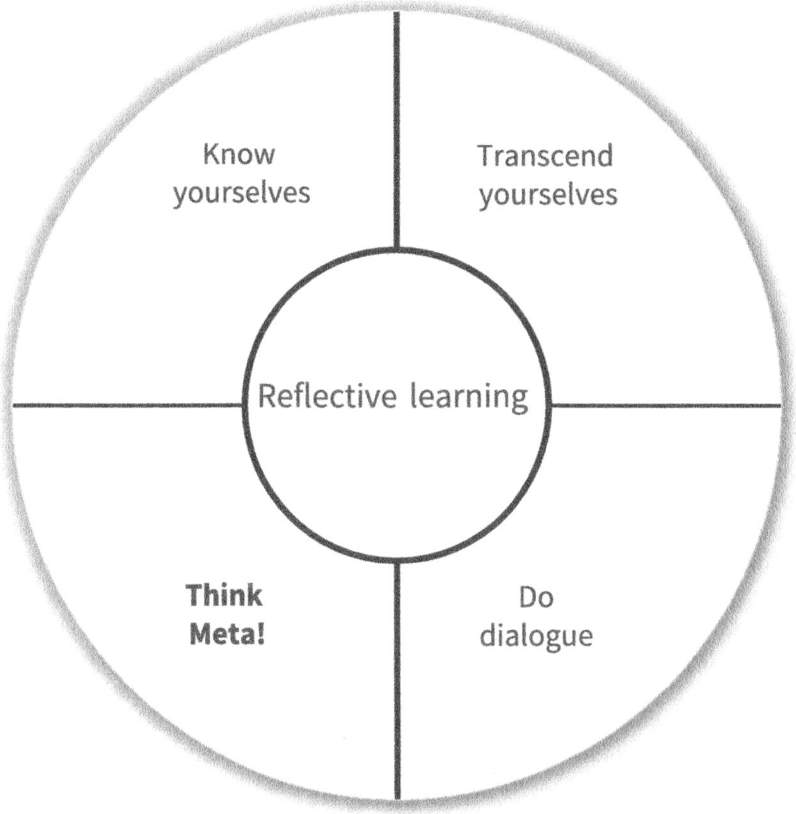

DOI: 10.4324/9781003284826-5

A leadership myth

Leadership is About Being in Control

Two years ago, Tony's manufacturing division experienced a major accident in one of its US plants. Reading an initial report as to what went wrong, Tony saw that people at the plant made several poor decisions, the outcomes of which combined with disastrous consequences. There was a major explosion in one of the core processing plants which killed three people and injured many more. The explosion caused fires that swept the rest of the facility, destroying it entirely. Local residents retreated indoors as the sky filled with black clouds and ash, the residue that covered roads, buildings, and parks. Residents wanted to know if the gases and ash were toxic and protested to the government to have the plant closed down permanently. The company had to pay out millions of dollars not only to rebuild the plant but to reassure authorities that the accident couldn't happen again.

Reading the report Tony identified three areas that had to be improved. First, processes and procedures had not been properly reviewed and updated since the integration of new technologies into safety systems. Second, processes and procedures were not always adhered to anyway. Third, management at the plant didn't appear to have carried out adequate system reviews and/or had not reported the results of those reviews regularly to head office.

Tony interviewed every member of the local executive team personally, to share his findings and seek explanations. The first two leaders he interviewed spoke at length as to how difficult it had been to review policy and procedure with existing resources, and to implement existing processes with newly reduced staffing levels. When asked why they hadn't raised these issues before, they said that they had raised the issues several times but had been told they needed to manage within existing budgets. Tony became impatient. He challenged the people he spoke to hard, refuting their arguments and labelling their performance as unacceptable. No one proved able to engage him in adequate debate. Their thinking was flawed and lazy, and their capacity to make a logical, rationale argument poor.

Tony set up a project team to address all three issues and to review operations at the remaining plants in the division. The team discovered similar issues across the business and recommended to Tony that more resources be deployed to check that remedial actions were implemented at every plant. Tony signed off on the recommendation, and on the compulsory redundancies of twelve leaders across the network.

Then Tony received a phone call telling him there had been a major accident at another plant on the west coast of the US. This time a major chemical leak into local waterways, attributable to corroding pipelines. Tony put his hands over his face and took several deep breaths. The next six months were going to be hell.

Theory

So far, we have defined wisdom in terms of a leader's commitment to learning, the extent to which a leader is selves-aware, and the extent to which a leader is able to transcend his or her selves. To self-transcend is to approach the world in a fundamentally different way. It is to recognize that everything we do impacts what others do and what others do impacts what we do. It is to recognize that how we think influences how others think, and how they think influences how we think. If we now consider this way of thinking in an organizational context, how does the self-transcendent leader think about change? The wisdom literature doesn't often talk about literature in a business context, but it does suggest that wise leaders:

- Recognize the limitations of their own knowledge[1]
- Are therefore humble[2]
- Appreciate the significance of a holistic perspective[3]
- Acknowledge uncertainty[4]
- Tolerate ambiguity[5]

All of this means that wise leaders know that they do not get to control the world around them. Judith Gluck suggests that most people have control illusions, a belief that they can control aspects of their lives that they cannot control[6]. This belief enables them to feel secure and happy. Wise individuals, she suggests, understand how unstable, uncertain, and uncontrollable the world is. They know that something bad may happen at any time, events they cannot control, but they are not anxious. Instead, they focus on what is good in life and trust in their capacity to engage with others in managing whatever may come along. They trust their ability to *influence* outcomes.

This leader recognizes the social process through which people make meaning of the world and form intentions. This leader is genuinely interested in what other people think, aware there is much she doesn't know. This is not to equate wisdom with ignorance; rather it is to equate wisdom with a recognition that we are ignorant and a desire to understand more. *'The fool doth think he's wise, but the wise man knows himself to be a fool'*[7]. The wise leader is unlikely to declare herself wise because she is constantly aware of what she doesn't know, and uncertain of what to do next. At the same time, she is curious and keen to learn, always testing new hypotheses and seeking to understand more through the outcome of those experiments. She does this in collaboration with others. Socrates framed wisdom as a collective endeavour[8]. How can one person alone hope to view the world other than through a subjective lens, a lens subject to unconscious bias?

Ancient schools of thought emphasized the recognition of uncertainty as a core aspect of being wise and, significantly, the role of conversation in attaining wisdom[9]. The wise leader understands the functioning of the social process through which new insights emerge. The wise leader is therefore curious, curious all the time as to what others are thinking and saying. She makes the time to bring others together into the same setting so that they might interact and generate something new through their interaction.

In Part Four we consider how the wise leader approaches change. This is important because leaders exist, essentially, to effect change. That might be the early in career leader wanting her sales team to focus more on the needs of our clients, or the more experienced leader trying to restructure a whole organization and make it more profitable. How a leader seeks to effect change depends on her philosophy of change. Some leaders focus on delivering a strong message and following up with people each day every day to make sure changes are implemented. These leaders often come across as busy, active, and sometimes emotional. Other leaders are more relaxed. They seem to spend less of their own time driving change, but the change seems to happen, nevertheless. What are these leaders doing differently?

In this section, we'll review five different ways of thinking about change[10], five different philosophies, and frame those different ways of thinking in terms of wisdom. We'll talk about what we call linear and non-linear approaches to change, and collaborative and complex approaches to change, before describing the meta-perspective. You will recognize all these approaches, certainly the linear and non-linear approaches. To what extent, however, will you identify with the meta-perspective? We believe all five approaches serve the leader well in certain contexts, but to successfully navigate complexity, the wise leader needs to able to access the meta-perspective.

In describing these five ways of thinking we talk about different ways of thinking about systems. The leadership literature is slowly being infiltrated by exhortations to think systemically. Over the last few years, in a world in which organizations must dedicate more of their energies to working across national boundaries, in which technology enables us to work ever faster and more efficiently, in which multiple stakeholders with often conflicting interests seek to push their agendas, so we hear more about the need to think systemically. But what does it mean to think more systemically? The term is rarely well-defined. Dissecting the popular narrative around systems and systems thinking, thinking more systemically seems to mean little more than taking a breath, stepping back, and looking at the bigger picture. This is often a useful thing to do. But the world of systems thinking offers further insights as to how we might benefit from thinking 'systemically', insights that help us clarify how the wise leader thinks.

Reviewing the academic narrative around systems and systems thinking, we come to realize that there are many different ways of thinking about systems and therefore change. These theories encourage us to do more than just stand back and access a more holistic perspective. They invite us to consider that broader view through particular lenses. Some of these lenses encourage us to try and change the 'system' by focusing on our message and trying to persuade others to understand the value of our message. Other lenses encourage us to take a different approach.

In this section, we present a simplified account of the myriad of systems theories that currently exist. We have sorted those theories into five buckets. None of these buckets are necessarily better than any of the other buckets, but the more buckets we have access to, the more agile and adaptable we are likely to be as a leader. The wise leader has access to all five ways of thinking and is able to 'think meta'.

Five ways of thinking about systems and change

1 Linear systemic

Through this lens, people think in simple linear terms about change. This is an approach to change based on pulling switches and levers. If I press the right button on my gas oven, a flame lights up. If I open my fridge door, a light comes on. If I press the right button on my remote, the garage door opens, or the television changes channel. This is a simple cause-and-effect model of change, and we see people thinking through this lens all the time. For example, people in the UK who said that if the government stopped contributing so much money to the European budget, it would have the same amount of money available to spend on health services. Or people who thought climate change would be about slightly higher temperatures and water levels, rather than whole new patterns of weather. Or people who thought they could stop COVID from getting into their country solely by imposing travel bans.

This way of thinking is enough to understand some of the problems we face in the workplace. If, for example, John is unhappy because he feels undervalued and unappreciated, then his demeanour may quickly change if he is given a promotion, a bigger desk, and featured in the in-house company magazine. Unfortunately, this way of thinking is not always enough. John's feelings about his role may be based on the way some of his colleagues talk to him, or deeply held beliefs about the way people behave in a workplace. He may not like the idea of being in a magazine. The promotion and the desk may have little impact.

We can characterize this approach to leadership as *controlling*. The leader sees the organization as a system, much like a hot water system, a system that she can stand apart from, diagnose, and adjust, in service of a desired outcome. If the hot water system is producing only cold water, then I need to replace the thermostat. If staff in the organization are unhappy then this must be remedied because we all know that levels of staff engagement correlate with sales and revenue. To lift staff morale all we need to do is to send a long list of questions to people, then act based on what the survey results tell us. The leader can control levels of staff engagement and thereby control sales and revenue. This leader likely behaves in a directive manner, issuing instructions and expecting those instructions to be carried out by more junior people in the organization. When things break down and things don't go to plan it's because there is a fault in the system, one or more cogs in the wheel (people) not doing what they're paid to do.

This linear systemic way of thinking is very common. The leader who thinks and behaves in this way may think of themselves as systemic – and they are systemic, because they are standing back, looking at the organization as a whole as if it is a system (a hot water system), and taking actions to tweak the system. These leaders may be encouraged in their approach to change by many of the books and texts written about change management. There are lots of change models, many like the diagram below (Figure 4.1).

This is the 'Kotter Model', and it lays out a linear sequence of steps the change leader must take to successfully implement change[11]. Notice how the model encourages the leader to adopt an expert role in determining the status quo and what needs to happen next. The leader corrals a few other leaders

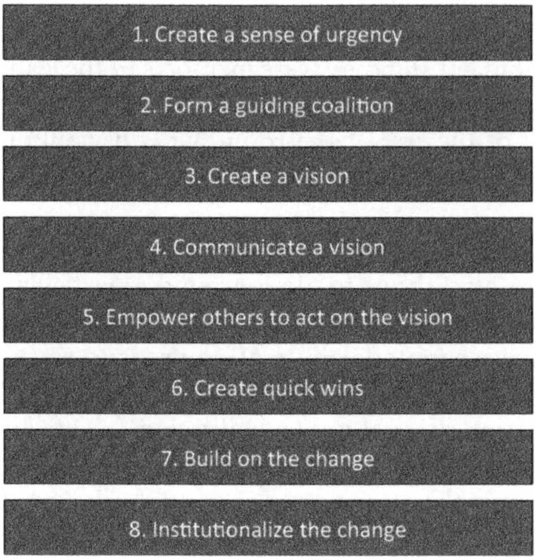

Figure 4.1 The Kotter Model of Change.

and between them they create a new vision for the company. They then *communicate* this vision, as in they tell everyone else what the vision is. Communication through this lens is a one-way process, not a two-way exchange of views. Watching leaders behave this way, based on a linear systemic way of thinking, we see people invited to attend workshops, ostensibly to decide what to do. But the important decisions have already been made.

> Shaun was invited to Brussels, along with 100 other leaders of the business for which he worked. The Head of European Operations opened the two-day meeting, explaining that their mission was to decide on a new operating model. They had a choice – they could choose to become a customer-centric organisation, or an operationally efficient organisation. The 100 leaders were asked to break out into groups of six or seven, each group facilitated by one of the leadership team. Each group was invited to decide – should we become customer-centric or operationally efficient? It became apparent to most people in the room that they were expected to choose operational efficiency.
>
> After lunch the whole group convened again and the Head of European Operations talked about how, in his view, adherence to operational efficiency would give them a competitive advantage in the marketplace. Then he asked everyone to stand up. Shaun was at the front of the room and stood up with everyone else. Then the Head of Operations asked people to sit down if they agreed that operational efficiency would give them a competitive advantage. Shaun remained standing while he thought about the competition. They were all already focussed on operational efficiency, weren't they? How would operational efficiency give them a competitive advantage? As he pondered, he suddenly realised he was the only person still standing. Everyone behind him had sat down. The only people in the room left standing were members of the leadership team, stood by the walls, encircling the 100 leaders. One of the leadership team asked Shaun, in front of the rest of the room, what it would take for him to sit down. Shaun, meantime, just wanted to sit down without looking silly.

Many change programs include workshops and other such events. People are invited to these workshops to align around a particular course of action. Although the facilitator is there to help people work together, the facilitator has already decided where the conversation needs to end up; it needs to end up aligned around the centrally driven intended change. We call this *facipulation*; manipulation dressed up as facilitation[12]. This approach to change is linear systemic, based on a principle that leaders know best. They know best because the way the system works is relatively simple, and they have access to all the data, so what's to talk about?

This way of thinking is sometimes enough. Want to sell more packets of washing powder? Spending more money on advertising might work. But often this way of thinking is not enough. Sometimes leaders have overlooked something in their quest to simplify what is going on. Others in the organization intuitively understand that the proposed solution won't work, but no one will listen to them, so they stop objecting. They stop objecting, but they don't engage enthusiastically in implementing the grand solution, and progress slows. Their leaders then get annoyed and frustrated and start complaining about middle management – they are too inert, too slow, too dull-witted. Leadership gets frustrated because they can't see what's going on through any other lens than the linear systemic lens. They get frustrated and annoyed and emotional, and no one thinks they are wise.

The linear systemic lens is sometimes sufficient. If I, as a leader, am charged only with achieving relatively simple, short-term goals, then this simple cause-and-effect philosophy may serve me well. I don't like uncertainty. I seek to control. I am not humble. I rely on tried and trusted methodologies. I don't see the need to collaborate, believing in my own intelligence to work out solutions. If this is the only lens I have access to, however, I am likely to come unstuck. I am not wise. I believe in my own individual agency and become frustrated when others appear to thwart that agency. I show up to others as individualistic, self-absorbed, anxious, and irritable.

2 Non-linear systemic

Wise leaders recognize the world is complex and understand the limitations of thinking in terms of simple cause and effect[13]. Through the non-linear systemic lens, people still think in terms of cause and effect, but they recognize that the world is complicated. Sometimes the relationship between cause and effect is curvilinear, not linear. Sometimes an action leads to a consequence that triggers another action.

For example, John still feels undervalued and unappreciated. He shares his feelings with Yu Dan, voicing his frustration with year-end assessment processes and pay scales. She agrees with everything he says and shares with him her own experiences and the experiences of other colleagues. John leaves the conversation even more frustrated. Over the next couple of weeks, he sees more flaws in the system and becomes more annoyed. He meets again with Yu Dan, who is also becoming more annoyed and frustrated. Each time they meet they are more convinced that the way the organization operates is unjust. Others are drawn into their narrative and people start leaving. Within six months the organization is seriously understaffed. Those people left behind are working longer hours, leaving them feeling even more disengaged and unhappy.

A leader thinking about reward and morale through a linear systemic lens would be at a loss to understand what was going on. Sure, if we're paying people a little under the odds, then we may have some discontent, and a few people may leave. But that's not what happened here. Positive feedback loops emerged; whereby discontent fed discontent and relatively low levels of discontent escalated quickly. People became so unhappy that people started leaving the organization in big numbers. Then a second positive feedback loop was created, whereby just one or two people missing in a team meant that people had to work exponentially harder to get the work done. Events moved quickly on from a few people being unhappy with reward processes, to the organization finding itself in crisis. The leader will only grasp what's happening if she is able to look at events through a *non*-linear systemic lens, recognizing the existence of self-reinforcing positive feedback loops.

A leader looking at life through a non-linear systemic lens would be more alert to John's unhappiness and more curious as to the causes. Instead of assuming he just wanted a promotion and a new desk, Tony wants to understand more about what is going on. He notices how much time John spends with Yu-Dan and gets to know Yu-Dan a little better too. He listens carefully to John and hears stories about his previous workplace and what he most valued about working in that organization. He realizes how much John values fairness. John has heard stories about the end-of-year assessment process, and how arbitrary the process is, in some people's eyes. Tony notices that Yu-Dan feels the same way and takes the time to understand their both feelings and to convey his concerns to those responsible for implementing the process. He gains assurances and conveys those assurances to John and Yu-Dan. John and Yu-Dan are appeased for a while, but their dissatisfaction doesn't go away and reappears with twice the energy soon after.

This approach to leadership is still controlling and the approach of the leader may still be quite hierarchical. The leader still sees the organization as a system, just a more complicated system. This system has some different circuits in it whose functioning needs to be highlighted and understood if the leader is to understand the functioning of the whole system. This leader takes more time to consider apparently simple issues and shows up to other people as being highly intelligent. She values intelligence in others and tends to consult with those she considers to be intelligent. Once she has worked out the complications of an issue to her satisfaction then she lets people know what they need to do and expects those instructions to be followed.

This non-linear systemic way of thinking is often required because few important issues are straightforward and linear. Why then do leaders often persist in linear systemic thinking rather than non-linear thinking? The barrier is often time. Organizations continue to get busier and busier. Time is of the essence. Leaders don't stop to look beyond the most obvious explanation. But the non-linear systemic perspective isn't always enough either.

As we said in the introduction to this section, there are many ways of thinking about systems, and some authors seek to establish a name for themselves by presenting *definitive* accounts of systems thinking, in the same way, that people try and position themselves as the definitive voice of leadership or coaching or strategy. Beware people who talk about systems thinking as if there is only one way of thinking about systems (just as you should beware authors writing about wise leadership as if their perspective is the only perspective!). One of the most popular proponents of systems thinking in the leadership literature has been Peter Senge and colleagues, who wrote the *Fifth Discipline* and the *Fifth Discipline Fieldbook*[14]. The authors describe five disciplines of an effective learning organization, the fifth of which is 'systems thinking'. They outline in great detail what they mean by systems thinking, presenting a series of models and frameworks that became very popular. But their perspective on systems thinking is quite a narrow version of systems thinking. As they state clearly in the *Fifth Discipline Fieldbook,* their ideas and frameworks derive from 'system dynamics', a particular theory of systems developed by colleagues at MIT. As David Lane and Mike Jackson say:

> "'I learned my systems thinking from Senge', runs the corollary, 'I don't need to repeat the process'. This is false. Being able to do systems thinking in the style of Senge, or even in the style of Forrester, is not the same as the approaches offered by other systems thinkers."[15]

Lane also says:

> "Systems dynamics is an element of the broad field of systems thinking. Yet usage of the term "systems thinking" to describe our own single methodology is virtually to deny the existence of any other. If we use that term for our one discipline, we are putting ourselves in a mental prison."[16]

We make this point now because many of the ideas expressed by Senge under the heading of 'systems thinking' are examples of non-linear systems thinking. They are useful ideas, but not the only ideas, and some of these ideas have been much critiqued when relied upon to address complex problems.

Like the linear systemic perspective, the non-linear systemic perspective encourages us to stand back and look for cause and effect. I am an *intelligent* leader and may be well known for being able to think out of the box and come up with imaginative solutions to difficult problems. If the leader's diagnosis of events is sufficient to move ahead effectively, then this leader may show up as smart, and lots of people associate being wise with being smart. But if her diagnosis doesn't do the job, then like the linear-systemic thinker, she is likely to come across as individualistic, self-absorbed, anxious, and irritable. This leader may also come across as scary, nimble on her feet in disputing others' views with impeccable logic, dismissing other people's ideas as undercooked, or just plain dumb.

3 Collaborative systemic

Gregory Bateson, an anthropologist, got excited when he was told that frogs can only see things that move. They can see flies flying and the rushes blowing in the wind, but they can't see stationary objects. To them, those objects don't exist. Bateson got excited because he saw parallels between the way people perceive the world and how their perception determines their thinking.

For example, Tony sees John is unhappy. He hears him complain about how unfair the end-of-year assessment system is. He initially frames the issue as being about John's values and previous experience in another organization. Through a collaborative systemic lens, however, he is humble. He doesn't assume he understands exactly what is going on. He recognizes what he sees and reminds himself there may be things going on he cannot see. Tony talks informally to other members of his leadership team. The leadership team come up with a collective hypothesis as to what motivates John, and what makes him feel appreciated and underappreciated. Faith, for example, has been paying attention to John's choice of words on occasion. She recognizes some of the phrases he uses from books, podcasts, and Ted Talks featuring a particular author on Human Resources. She explains some of that author's ideas and Tony begins to understand the extent to which John has been influenced by that author. Ursula knows the town where John was born. It's a town in the south of England that has voted liberal for 30 years, surrounded by other districts that always vote conservative. The local football team is owned by the fans. The local cinema is publicly owned. All the pubs serve beer from the local brewery. This was all news to Tony. Between them, Tony, Faith, and Ursula build a more complete picture of what may be going on for John and a plan for helping him become happier and more engaged.

This way of thinking demands humility. It requires us to recognize the limitations of our own individual capacity to understand complex issues. But not all leaders are taught to be humble. Some leaders are taught to be smart and decisive. They evolve believing that leaders are supposed to know all the answers. They have worked in organizations where it is not OK to say, *'I'm not sure'*, or *'I don't know'*, or *'I need to discuss that with my team'*. These leaders are unlikely to accept the invitation to look at events through a collaborative systemic lens because they are committed to their own intelligence and the power of logic and rational thinking.

Notice that this approach to leadership is still based on a philosophy of control. The leader still sees the organization as a system, albeit a system whose functioning is impossible to objectively analyse. The leader through this lens, makes time to address complex problems and consults with others. This leader is humbler, recognizing that there are at least some people in the community whose views are worth understanding. But ultimately this leader still thinks of change in terms of personal influence and decision-making and may still think in terms of organization as a hierarchy.

Again, sometimes this way of thinking serves us well and sometimes it doesn't. This leader may show up as wise through her capacity to engage and collaborate. But she may show up as less wise if agreed-upon solutions fail to achieve desired outcomes. The leader may then again become frustrated. That annoyance may be directed at some of the people whose views she solicited as well as herself – what did we miss? What did we get wrong? Remember this perspective is still based on a philosophy of control. If I believe in my capacity to control and I don't succeed in getting my way, then I become anxious or annoyed and people tend to equate wisdom with being calm.

4 Complex systemic

All three previous perspectives assume that the organization can usefully be compared to some kind of machine. The leader exercises control over her domain and her efforts to exercise that control can be readily assessed. The complexity perspective, on the other hand, views leadership behaviour in terms of influence, not control. Through the complex system lens, the leader may enjoy positional power, but that doesn't mean they have control.

In the book *Leading Change*[17], we tell the story of the CEO of a South African organization who made a personal commitment to transforming the way his company operated. He engaged with people across the business, unions, and local communities to develop a charter, from which were borne various projects and initiatives. The program started but wasn't successful because the leader hadn't successfully engaged others on his leadership team.

Having total engagement at the leadership team level doesn't guarantee success either.

> Rob was charged with introducing a new sales process through a retail organisation. He had the full support of the leadership team who were excited by the results at a pilot site. Based on those results they all believed that if every staff member became skilled at on-selling, then revenue numbers would increase 10–15%. Rob shared the results with district sales managers, who scheduled staff training sessions at every retail site. Six months later the entire workforce was trained, but sales results were disappointing. They had spent over a million dollars on training, but revenues had hardly shifted. At Rob's request, members of the senior leadership team visited sites to reiterate the importance of on-selling. Mystery shoppers were deployed to check staff were complying with the new sales technique. Still nothing shifted. Relatively few staff were actively on-selling and those who did, did so reluctantly. The senior leadership team started putting pressure on district manager and site managers. Some people lost their jobs. But still revenues didn't shift. Eventually management attention turned to a new initiative.

So, what happened? In this case, had the senior leadership team been curious, they would have discovered that customers didn't like being on-sold to. Sales may have gone up at the pilot site, but that didn't mean that customer satisfaction went up too. Customers were unhappy, and sales staff had been recruited for their capacity to empathize.

The linear systemic perspective wasn't helpful here. On-selling would be regarded as a lever, which when pulled would yield more revenue. There was no logical reason why staff weren't pulling the lever. The non-linear perspective wasn't useful either. Sure, we might work out that staff weren't happy on-selling because they didn't like to disappoint customers, but a belief in positional power and control would still have leadership trying to pull levers. The collaborative systemic perspective probably wouldn't work either because no matter how many perspectives Rob accessed; he would still ultimately be seeking to persuade staff to on-sell in order to drive business revenues. All these perspectives share an underlying belief in the leader's capacity to make things happen and control outcomes.

The complexity perspective recognizes that leaders don't get to control outcomes and that change emerges through a complex web of social interaction. These processes cannot be controlled but they can be influenced.

> Rob put aside his anxieties about the general reluctance to on-sell. He went out to sites to observe what was happening and to ask a lot of questions. Staff got to know him and trust him. At some sites, staff were on-selling. They listened to their manager and to the district manager and understood how they could increase revenues through on-selling. Lots of customers didn't much like being on-sold to, but they were making more money and that was their job.
>
> At other sites there was more tension. Some staff were willing to on-sell, others were not. They saw their role as being to drive customer satisfaction. On-selling might increase revenues in the short-term, but it would lose the company clients in the longer term, and it was no fun trying to sell people services they didn't want. At most of these sites an uneasy truce seemed to have been arrived at. If everyone on shift was happy to on-sell, then everyone on-sold. If just one or two people on shift were not happy to on-sell, then no one on-sold.
>
> At other sites no one wanted to on-sell and so no-one did. At district meetings people from on-selling sites mixed with people from sites that didn't on-sell and sites where some people on-sold and other didn't. In one of those districts the emerging narrative was that the company didn't understand what customers really wanted but staff needed to make some kind of attempt to on-sell in order to ensure no one lost their job. In a nearby district the narrative was different – head office knew what they were doing, but too many staff were not 'commercial'. In another district on-selling made no sense, and staff had started collecting images of the people they though were the mystery shopper and on-selling only to those people.

Rob is thinking differently now. He knows he cannot control sales staff behaviours. He has put aside his agenda and gone out into the network only curious and determined to understand. He notices that people in different locations have made different sense of the edict to on-sell. People talk all the time about the on-selling drive with their local colleagues. Every site is different and so every site has come up with its own conclusions as to what the edict means and how they should respond. People from different sites mingle with each other at district meetings and have different conversations. Local narratives mix with other local narratives to create a new broader narrative. Change, Rob realizes, is in a state of constant flux, mediated by a thousand conversations between different people with different ways of looking at the world. He understands that there is no single message that will persuade all these people to start on-selling. He realizes that if people ever are to on-sell, then all their perspectives will need to be understood and addressed by senior management if they are to have any influence on outcomes.

It was big news in Sydney in March 2020, when locals flocked to Bondi Beach on a sunny day in the middle of the COVID lockdown, ignoring social-distancing rules. Authorities were outraged. David Elliott, a government minister, was quoted as saying:

> "What we saw this morning at Bondi Beach was the most irresponsible behaviour of individuals that we've seen so far. This is not something we are doing because we are the fun police. This is about saving lives."[18]

Over the course of the pandemic, it was intriguing to see the same behaviour manifest in other countries around the world. It happened on Manhattan Beach, in the USA, in April 2020. A representative of the city council said:

> "It is imperative that we continue to remind our community in the strongest possible terms that social distancing requirements must be followed. Those who are not taking this seriously will be cited."[19]

In May 2020, beachgoers flooded the Ozarks, in Missouri, USA. The local mayor, Lyda Krewson, said:

> "It's irresponsible and dangerous to engage in such high-risk behaviour just to have some fun over the extended holiday weekend. Now, these folks will be going home to St. Louis and counties across Missouri and the Midwest, raising concerns about the potential of more positive cases, hospitalisations, and tragically, deaths. Deeply disturbing."

It happened in Bournemouth, in the UK, in June 2020. MP Tobias Ellwood was reported as saying:

"A lot of people have chosen to be not just irresponsible but dangerous. We've made such progress tackling this pandemic. I'd hate to see Bournemouth be the one place in Britain that gets that second spike."[20]

From the first three systemic perspectives these behaviours don't make sense. They are irrational and illogical. Those in authority are frustrated and think hard about how best to regain control of the situation. Through the complex systemic lens, the leader may still be concerned and frustrated, *and* is curious. These people that pack the beaches at a time of pandemic – what is the narrative here? How are these people making sense of what's happening? And, if I seek to influence the behaviour of these people, how do I find out what these people are thinking? Am I open to a different perspective? How can I craft my own message in a way that is more likely to be heard?

We did come across a lovely example of this way of thinking in action during COVID. We spoke to someone on the board of a dance company in North America. She spoke about how the company sought to stay open by enforcing social distancing rules. Then a group of dancers got together for someone's birthday party and enough people contracted COVID to close the company down. The person we spoke to was frustrated but also curious and compassionate. She reflected on how many of the dance company were young people living alone and away from home. She reflected that many of them had few strong friendships in the area and recognized how much they must have yearned social interaction. She spoke of conversations taking place across the company to better understand the issue in service of managing it better in the future.

Let's return to Tony and John. Through this complex systemic lens, Tony stops thinking so much about John as a discrete issue to be managed. He finds out more about the end-of-year assessment process and reward policy. He explores the origin of these schemes and discovers who are advocates, who are sceptics, and who seem indifferent. He explores how others feel about these schemes more broadly, not just John and Yu-Dan. He talks to the people asked to administer the process each month and what they do to try and make the process equitable. He asks what are the obstacles and barriers? By the time he is finished he has a much better understanding of the process and how it works, some of the factors that get in the way of the process working well, and how the current pattern of conversations in the business serve to maintain the status quo, for now. He forms some hypotheses as to how the system might operate more effectively and starts sharing those views with others in the system, always curious as to how others make sense of what she says. Through these conversations new possibilities emerge, new ways of doing things she thinks enough people may happily align around.

This way of thinking constitutes a very different approach to leadership. Through this lens the leader recognizes she cannot step aside from her organization and view it as a machine. She cannot invite others to stand outside the organization with her in collective diagnosis. She herself is a *part* of the system that she seeks to lead. Just as she reflects from time to time on the nature of the organization and how it is operating, so do others. The conversations she has with members of her team are just a few of many conversations taking place across the organization. Her private thoughts and the conversations she engages with take place within the organization – they form part of the fabric of the organization just as all the other private thoughts and conversations do. If there is a machine, then she is as much part of it as anyone else. The diagnoses she makes, the conversations she has, all take place within that system.

This leader recognizes that she cannot control events. She is less likely to think in terms of simple hierarchy. She can however influence events – indeed everything she says and does influence events. And what others do and say also influences outcomes. This leader appears avidly curious, determined to get out and engage, to listen and to speak her mind. When she speaks her mind, she doesn't expect people to agree with her or to bend to her will. Instead, she is curious to see how others respond, curious to learn from their perspectives, and ready to speak her mind again. This leader is wiser.

We see less evidence of this way of thinking because the biggest barrier to this way of thinking is letting go of the idea of control. We all like to feel in control and in organizations we are encouraged to feel we have control. We are asked to commit to certain outcomes, including financial outcomes, and if we don't deliver on those outcomes, it is not usually acceptable to shrug and blame complexity.

5 Meta-systemic thinking

This approach is similar in principle to the complexity approach. The difference is that the meta-systemic practitioner recognizes that boundaries are not real. Advocates of complexity thinking often talk about systems and sub-systems, or nested systems. The organization is a system, functions are sub-systems and the teams within those functions are sub-sub-systems. Change happens at a local level as people within these sub-systems make their own meaning of events, and these meanings surface to intersect with other meanings, from which emerge high-level patterns of thought, conversation, and behaviour. But organizations are not systems, not in the sense of being comparable to hot water systems, aircraft engines, living systems, or weather systems.

One might describe an organization as a social system, but organizations are not social systems either because organizations are just mental constructs. Teams are mental constructs too. One of the questions a team coach will often ask individuals on a team before the coaching starts is – who's on the team? People often give different answers. The EA who is there to take notes is on the team according to some people, not others. The CFO's number two, who is always present when anything to do with numbers is discussed, is on the team according to some people, not others. When working with teams what we have is who is in the room at the time, and that group often changes from session to session. So why do we talk about teams? Because people like to belong. Organizations and teams are mental constructs that we characterize and personify. If the characterization is positive and enabling, then it is attractive, and people want to belong to the team and/or organization. The characterization is useful because it encourages engagement and commitment.

But teams and organizations are just mental constructs. An organization is real in that there is a legal body to whom some of us are contracted to work, but that's about it. When you walk around an office building, who do you see? Some of those people are contracted to the 'organization'. Some are long term contractors. Some are short-term contractors. Some are visitors. We are not seeing the 'organization'. The organization, strictly speaking, is a group employed under contract. Those contracts are often quite different in terms of duration, remuneration, and conditions. Yet we interact with everyone we need to in order to get our work done, whether they are contracted to the organization or not. We create this notion of organization as something real again because people like to belong. You see people wearing t-shirts with the company logo on it that says – look at me – I belong to xyz. It's a happy simplification that enables us to easily characterise the place where we work. We talk about organizations as if they are real entities, with their own personalities, attributes, strengths, and weaknesses. When we do that, we are creating a mental construct, a construct that enables us to make simple that which we experience at work What do you think of when you think of companies like Enron, Google, BP, and Pfizer? The personalities we ascribe to these organizations are mental constructs, based on what we have heard people say about these organizations.

So, what? you may ask.

Well, if we over-invest in any of these systems metaphors, if we over-invest in the idea of the organization-as-system, with its sub-systems and sub-sub-systems, then we may over-privilege the role people in the organization/division/team play, and under-privilege the role others play. For example, a lot of team coaches focus on the dynamics within a team and invite team members to take greater ownership of those dynamics. This may be a useful thing to do. However, it may not be a useful thing to do if people are distracted from considering the impact of conversations with people outside the 'team' on relationships within the team.

The people we engage with in our lives are members of a vast social network. The conversations we have with people in that network influence how we think and what we do. That includes friends, family, and the people we talk to on the touchline watching our kids play their sport. It includes the barista we talk to every morning at the coffee shop, the taxi driver, and the newsagent. It includes customers and suppliers and people from other parts of the 'organization' I find myself talking to at the pub every Friday. The drawback of the complex systemic perspective, as a metaphor, is that it may lead us to over-privilege relationships with people in the team, division, or organization and fail to sufficiently acknowledge the influence of people in the social network but not part of the organization.

Through this lens, Tony doesn't limit his exploration of end-of-year assessment processes and reward policies to conversations within the organization. Yes, he explores the origin of those schemes and discovers who are advocates, who are sceptics, and who seem indifferent. He explores how others in the organization feel about these schemes etc ... But in talking to all these people she wonders who else they are talking to? He asks people who they like to read and who they listen to. He engages with local industry bodies and associations, with popular narratives emerging through Ted Talks and so on. As he continues to explore, he finds himself thinking not only about John and his dissatisfaction with process and policy; he finds himself thinking more generally about the conversations he hears around him and the thousands of other conversations from which emerge many of the opinions and beliefs he encounters every day. He sees himself and John as active participants in that active social network and recognizes how unaware he usually is as to the way things really work. How everything seems to be articulated in terms of individual personality and behaviour.

We call this perspective the meta-systemic, not the anti-systemic, or the post-systemic. We call it the meta-systemic because we see all systemic perspectives as being useful but limited. We don't want to lose the value of the useful metaphor. We simplify things all the time, we look for ways of making the complex simple. This helps us to make decisions. And we need to recognize the limitations of those metaphors, which sometimes matter and sometimes don't.

Practically speaking, this way of thinking is not radically different from the complex systemic. The complex systemic way of thinking recognizes the emergence of meaning and intention through conversation. Change cannot be controlled; it can only be influenced. The meta-systemic perspective recognizes the value of this metaphor but ensures we pay attention to the fact that meaning-making processes span these imaginary organizational boundaries. People make sense of their world through *all* the conversations they have.

This leader is hungry to understand what others think, including people outside the organization. She doesn't identify in quite the same way with some of the values and stories that organizations tell themselves in order to generate cohesion, engagement, and alignment. She sees these boundaries and stories for what they are – often useful constructs that help us move ahead purposefully.

The wisdom literature tells us we don't get to control many aspects of our lives, despite some of us being otherwise deluded. The wise leader recognizes that sense-making and change are complex, unpredictable processes that she can only influence. She is humble and curious, keen to engage in the social processes she understands sit at the heart of change. Leaders who have access only to the first three ways of thinking may still be suffering from the illusions of control described by Judith Gluck[21]. If they are humble, they are humble only up to a point. They don't yet fully appreciate the social process through which change takes place, a process that can be influenced by anyone at any time. They may over-privilege models that simplify the way the world works and reduce strategy to an intellectual exercise. The wise leader is a skilled influencer, calm in the face of complexity, someone known for their propensity to listen to anyone, regardless of rank.

Epilogue

Tony Discovers Humility

Tony read the new report on the major chemical leak. It spoke again to inadequate policy and procedure, poor process, and poor communication. Tony knew the team that had been asked to prepare the report and understood how they operated. They moved onsite quickly, collated data, conducted interviews, then returned to head office to write their report. He had great respect for their work, but he suspected he would need to dig deeper to get a more in-depth understanding of what took place. What happened didn't make logical sense. He had taken a wholly logical approach to managing the disaster two years ago, an approach that hadn't worked.

This time Tony went to the site himself, taking with him a diverse team of people, comprising safety professionals and plant operators, including people from outside his division and outside the organization. Onsite, technical experts engaged with their counterparts from the plant and went through all available data. Tony engaged an external team of change academics to interview other people at the plant, making sure they spoke to everyone, from Chief Executive to the cleaners.

Tony took on the team someone who he trusted implicitly to tell him what she thought. Two reports now said that local management was reluctant to speak up. He recognized that one of his selves was energetic, determined, and action-oriented. He recognized another self was analytical and valued intelligence. These two selves working in cahoots weren't easy to engage with. They pushed forwards and listened only to people able to engage with them in a fast, furious, logical argument. These selves had often served him well in pushing forward with big projects, but when it came to the kind of complex problem he was facing now, he needed to bring forth his more thoughtful, curious self and his more empathic self. These gentler selves didn't always succeed in being heard by his action-oriented and analytical selves, and he sought support from Melanie in ensuring he stayed on track.

Tony and Melanie stayed on site for more than a fortnight. By the end of the two weeks a picture was emerging. Staff at the plant remembered a time when policy and processes were rigidly adhered to. For several years, however, requests to fix machinery in line with requirements were not responded to. Different teams in different parts of the plant compared notes and found that none of their requests were being met. Some groups attributed that to incompetent management. Others attributed it to the head office's unwillingness to provide adequate budget. Others thought it was because policies and procedures were under review and that maintenance funds were being ring-fenced until maintenance funds would be available once the review was completed. At the executive team level, the predominant story was that no one in the head office understood plant operations and received their requests for more money as evidence that they weren't good enough at doing their jobs. This meant they were reluctant to keep pushing back on head office, and reluctant to engage their own teams in conversation about what was really happening for fear they would look bad. The first major accident, two years ago, hadn't changed things. Their requests for a higher maintenance budget went unanswered. Instead, they had hundreds of new forms to fill in, testifying that they had implemented new policies, the functions of which were not clear to anyone in the plant.

At the end of the fortnight, Tony recognized that he needed to get much better at engaging in conversation with his plant managers. He needed to review the requirements for people brought into head office, making sure he achieved a much better balance of personnel in that area, valuing experience as much as he did pure intellect. He needed to ensure that people generally, including himself, got much better at building trusting relationships and stopping to listen to inconvenient truths.

Self-development

In Part Four we have reviewed different ways of thinking about systems. We don't ask you to decide which way of thinking you most identify with. Instead, we invite you to consider which ways of thinking you most identify with in what contexts. Which part of you identifies with the meta-systemic way of thinking? When might you want to call more upon that part of you, when other ways of thinking don't seem to be working? And if none of your parts lean toward the meta-systemic, which of your selves might be the best candidate to further explore the possibility that a meta-systemic perspective might be helpful?

We believe we can all show up wise in certain contexts. We feel humble and calm and capable of making good decisions. But in other contexts, we feel less humble and more emotional. How do we become more agile and able to manage a greater diversity of situations and contexts?

You will have done most of the hard work required to *think meta* in the first three parts of this book. To think meta is to view the world around us as one dynamic ever-shifting network of people, constantly in relationship with each other. This is almost inevitably how you think about the world anyway if you have achieved levels of self-transcendence. The suggested actions for Part Four of the book are more practical, intended to help you plan your next big change intervention more clearly, and to challenge some of the things others may be saying to you about effective change leadership. As we said earlier, the purpose of leadership is ultimately about achieving positive change. Our ability to do this wisely is related to our ability to access a meta-systemic perspective.

1 Consider – how do you think now?

Think about some of your efforts to lead change. Think about specific examples, important moments at which you had to decide what to do next. How were you thinking at that time? You can probably come up with examples of approaching change through several of the five lenses if not all of them.

Linear systemic	Searching for the simple lever. Expecting that if I do *this*, then *that* will happen.
Non-linear systemic	Spending a bit more time looking for the less obvious lever or levers. Knowing I need to spend some time thinking about what *this* is.
Collaborative systemic	Bringing a diverse of group together to compare perspectives. Working together to work out what *this* might be.
Complex systemic	Getting out into the organization to listen and understand. Fearlessly sharing your own view, unafraid of being challenged – indeed looking forward to being challenged, being curious. Letting go of your desire to control change, looking for what emerges through conversation with others.
Meta-systemic	Casting your net wider, beyond your organization, and engaging more broadly with others to navigate the issue. Letting go of your agenda and engaging in conversation with a truly diverse set of stakeholders, including those that may seem indifferent or resistant to your agenda.

Think about one or two specific examples of times when you led change. Which way of thinking best characterizes how you were thinking in those examples?

2 Think multiple

Shaun recognizes himself in all these modes. Is he wise – he asks himself? If so – from where within himself does this wisdom arise? He considers each of his five work-selves in turn and asks himself which form of systemic thinking does each of his selves appear to align with most easily? He thinks in terms of leanings, because it seems too black and white to suggest that each of his selves thinks the same way in every context (Table 4.1).

Reflecting on his responses, Shaun recognizes that it no longer seems meaningful to him to ask himself – am I wise? He doesn't show up as wise in every context and he may never do so. Many people who know him well would be unlikely to describe him as wise necessarily because they would see all his selves, some of which think through linear- and non-linear lenses. Others may think of him as wise because they see that wisdom at certain moments. It becomes clear to him how subjective is the term 'wise leader'. He

Table 4.1 Shaun's five work selves – systemic leanings

	Systemic leanings
Action Shaun	Toward linear systemic – desire to get things done quickly, feeling personally responsible for outcomes.
Playful Shaun	Toward collaborative systemic – desire to explore with others, looking forward to new insights emerging.
Loving Shaun	Toward complex systemic – desire to understand connectivity, putting self in other's shoes, seeking to understand what emerges from multiple relationships.
Focussed Shaun	Toward meta-systemic and a recognition that we grow and develop together. Noticing self evolve through relationships with others.
Self-critical Shaun	Moving from non-linear systemic and a belief that I need to be clever to succeed, to complex- and meta-systemic and the realization that being clever isn't enough. Recognizing that self is in transition, staying committed to the challenge.

is drawn more to a recognition that he believes that he is capable of being wise more often. From 'being wise' to 'being capable of being wise' feels like an important distinction. He realizes that wisdom is the journey and not the destination.

3 When and how might you think differently?

Review your list of specific examples from your answer to the first question. Reflecting on those scenarios, what insights emerge for you if you attempt to consider the scenario through alternative lenses, such as the complex systemic or meta-systemic perspectives? If those insights are useful, how might you enhance your capacity to access those perspectives in-the-moment? This is a more powerful exercise when actioned through a multiplicity lens.

Shaun reflects on his notes and sees how unlikely it is that Action Shaun will make wise decisions in a complex situation. Action Shaun likes to get things done quickly. He looks for obvious solutions, seizes upon them, and gets things done. Playful Shaun enjoys collaboration and is genuinely interested in what others think, as is Loving Shaun. Loving Shaun is more likely to reflect on the nature of that connectivity and patterns of interaction. Focussed Shaun sees how his individual desire to grow and develop has emerged and continues to evolve from his interaction with others, including many people he has met through industry associations or online forums. Self-critical Shaun sees how an understanding of complex- and meta-systemic perspectives now raises the bar on what it means to be the person he wants to be. These realizations further help Shaun work out how to be wiser more often. For example, when Action Shaun is in full flow, but people are resisting his energy, he determines to call on Focused Shaun to help him reframe and review, before going again. Playful Shaun reminds himself not to get caught out by immersing himself in the fun. He needs to stay focussed on his purpose, his desire to lead change, and call on Focused Shaun when useful.

4 Influencing how others think

We talk a lot more about influencing in Part Five, but for now, we must answer the question we always get asked – what if I'm thinking meta, but no one else is?

If I'm thinking through a linear systemic lens, I'm looking for a lever I can pull to make everyone think the way I would like them to think. Through a non-linear systemic lens, I'm looking for a neat little strategy that will help me achieve the same outcome. It might have several components to it and might take me some time, but again I am looking for a roadmap to getting everyone to where I would like them to be. Through a collaborative systemic lens, I know the authors of this book won't be able to tell me what I need to do, but if I gather the right group of people together to consider the issue, between us we will come up with a strategy likely to achieve our desired outcome, which is everyone thinking meta and aligning around a change strategy we think is most likely to work.

The complex systemic approach has us thinking quite differently. We recognize that we are not sitting outside the system/organization. We are a part of it. We have all read the book and we like Part Four, which talks about thinking meta. We would like everyone in the organization to be thinking meta. We recognise also that Part Four of the book is just a perspective. It isn't 'true' – it is just another way of looking at change, someone else's simplification of how change works. We recognize that there are multiple ways of thinking about change and that there are other people, and other groups in our network thinking about change differently but with equal passion and sincerity. We don't seek to persuade all these people to think the way that we think. We seek to understand how they are thinking and how all these different ways of thinking come together at the macro level. We are above all curious, and keen to share our perspective as our perspective continues to evolve and change. We seek to understand how people are currently making sense of the world and we ask more questions when those answers don't make complete sense to us. We ask questions not to try and prove a point, but to challenge, to attempt to stimulate reflection and insight. We choose to engage in reflective learning when we are in dialogue with them, in order to enhance our own understanding of what might be possible. We are open to the possibility there is a different, better, way of thinking about systems than the ones outlined in this book.

Through the meta-lens, we also reflect the extent to which the systemic approach may be blinding us to the influence of others outside our team/division/organization.

- Whose views are most influential within the broader social network?
- Who do I need to engage with outside the organization if I am to most effectively influence how people inside the organization think?
- What other perspectives can I bring into these interactions to help us all move toward our collective futures?

Designing interventions

Part Four of this book builds on Parts One to Three. The extent to which it makes sense to you will likely depend on the extent to which previous sections make sense, particularly Part Three *transcend yourselves*. Some of you may already engage with the material around *think meta!* even if you haven't read or haven't fully engaged with the materials on *transcend yourselves*, but your engagement is most likely to be conceptual and intellectual. Understanding the material intellectually doesn't mean that the meta lens is how you habitually make sense of the world and so we do first encourage you to review your responses to Parts One, Two, and Three of this book before moving too quickly to Part Four. Once you are ready then we offer you the following guidance.

1 Have a view on change

There may be other people in your organization who have more formal responsibilities for leading change across your organization, but that doesn't mean you don't also have responsibilities for a change. If it is your role to facilitate the development of leadership in your organization, then it is your role to help those people enhance their capacity to lead change, because that is essentially what leaders do. So, it is important to ask yourself – how is it possible to help leaders become better at leading change without having your own philosophy on change or how change operates?

In Part One of the book, we encouraged you to be clear as to how you believe people most effectively learn. In Part Two we encouraged you to have a clear view of self, and the multiplicity of self. In Part Three we encouraged you to have a clear position on adult development and the nature of self-transcendence. Now we're suggesting you have a view on change. You may feel we are asking you to spend too much time reading books and understanding theory. And that may be; we do believe that people who head up disciplines such as leadership development ought to see it as part of their role to self-educate and keep up to speed with a constantly evolving literature on related subjects. We come across too many OD people who see their key roles as being project management, logistics, and delivery, neglecting the crucial contribution they can make to helping their organization understand what effective leadership development really looks like. Project management, logistics, and delivery are of course important, but we suggest that you also dedicate time to understanding some of the underlying theories underpinning leadership development and change. Many practitioners, in our experience, don't have a broad understanding of their discipline. Such people tend to be drawn to the latest popular book or podcast or Ted Talk. The problem with this is that much of what shows up in the leadership and change literature is populist, based more on individual conviction than any kind of evidence base. These unproven, albeit hugely popular perspectives, may engage and excite, but are unlikely to help you elevate the capacity of your leadership in any sustainable way. We encourage you to be discerning, and to be discerning requires that you invest at least some time in the theoretical. We often hear practitioners say that they need to be *practical* and not get bogged down in theoretical debate that none of their stakeholders are interested in. To those people, we suggest that it isn't a question of being theoretical *or* practical, it's a question of being both theoretical *and* practical. Of course, you need to be developing solutions that make sense to your organization, but these programs will be more effective the greater your personal commitment to reflective learning, the first of the five mantras of wise leadership.

We don't suggest that you rush out and immediately seek to be an 'expert' on everything leadership and change. First, that's not practical – the literature is vast. Second, beware of the desire to become an 'expert' anyway. There are multiple perspectives on leadership and change. What's important in our view is that you have an ongoing commitment to learning, that you always have a view that enables you to be discerning, and that you remain open always to new ways of thinking and doing.

So, our first suggestion to you as leaders in the leadership and change domains is to commit to an ongoing program of learning for yourself. We don't suggest you identify one course then use your learnings from that course as an ongoing reference point forever and a day. Instead, we encourage you to embrace the prospect of a lifelong learning journey, to be comfortable in not-knowing, and to include change in your learning agenda. What do you currently know about the nature of change? What else would you like to know about leading change? Do you feel you are progressed sufficiently along the journey to have a view that you feel confident sharing with people inside and outside your organization?

2 Role model

We suggest you consider the exercises we offered to your leaders in the Part Three. Those exercises are designed to help your leaders embrace the materials in a practical sense. We invite you to do those exercises yourselves. How do you currently think in practice? How might you think differently and in what contexts? How do you currently go about seeking to influence your organization in supporting the development of its leaders? You probably find that part of your role particularly challenging – most OD people do. Some of your key stakeholders don't think about leadership and change the way you do. Some of them may think in quite linear systemic terms, others non-linear, others collaborative, etc ... How will you seek to influence those people to allow you space to do the work you think will be most useful? What new conversations might you engage in now?

3 Embrace group coaching

Apologies if we start to sound like a one-track record, taking every opportunity to espouse the value of group coaching. However, some people find the material on systems overly conceptual and hard to translate into tangible action. The worst thing you can do is present this kind of material, then leave people to go and make sense of it by themselves. Everyone is busy these days, and if the material is too hard to interpret, then nothing gets done. If you are presenting this material as part of a workshop, then we advocate making *plenty* of time for people to make sense of the material together in practical terms. Part Five will help – *do dialogue*. Some people will understand the material faster than others. Those people can help the rest of the group. Work with small groups, no more than five or six people in each, so that everyone has time to flag questions and offer a perspective. Make time for those discussions rather than limit people to 10–15 minutes of discussion in service of getting through all your materials. Provide the resource for people to continue making sense of the materials, designing experiments, and comparing progress.

Group coaching, done well, feels spacious for participants. They don't experience being hurried through a rigid agenda, instead, they appreciate the space to decide where they want to go as a group, to explore and learn together. This requires patience and expertise of the group coach, who is adept at recognizing the learning needs of the group and crafting the space for them to explore those needs collectively. There is never a linear pathway with group coaching – rather it becomes an energetic dance, as groups grapple with new ways of thinking and collectively form realizations for themselves that they then take forward. The ability and propensity to engage in reflective learning (collectively and individually) sits at the heart of wise leadership.

4 Go l-o-n-g and support reflection

Again, we find ourselves repeating some of the principles from Parts One, Two, and Three. Again, these principles are essential when it comes to supporting leaders in leading change differently. The meta-approach to change will be counterintuitive for many people, particularly those committed to controlling change outcomes. You may have introduced them to the idea of *selves-awareness* and the *transcendence of selves*, but these ideas take time to explore and digest. So, many of your leaders may initially struggle with the idea that they don't get to control change. Many of your leaders believe it is their job to make things happen. They may place a lot of faith in positional power, or else put a lot of pressure on themselves in terms of their capacity to influence people to think what they want them to think. To commit to approaching some of their key deliverables fundamentally differently will take a lot of thought and courage. If some of your leaders are to really give it a go, then you need to support them over a period of time, and that support will likely include the opportunity to share insights and experiences with fellow leaders, creating new forums for communication as needed. You need to ensure they have the opportunity to reflect with others over an extended period of time and that they can call upon others with an experience in leading change, people who have successfully led change in the way that you advocate. Creating or enabling forums for collective reflection is critical to your change agenda.

Your 3Ps revisited

Let's look again at the 3Ps (Figure 4.2).

As a leader, what ideas have resonated for you in Part Four? For example, our suggestions that:

- All leaders think systemically
- We can identify five ways of thinking systemically
- Under pressure, we may lean toward a linear-systemic way of thinking, which doesn't always work
- If we over-privilege individual intelligence, we may not succeed in navigating complex change
- To manage complexity well requires letting go of a need for control and doubling down on our ability to influence inside and outside of our teams, divisions, and organizations.
- Wise leaders don't only think systemically, they think meta-systemically

How did our suggestions for self-development resonate with you in terms of challenging the way you think about change?

- What concrete steps will you take to become more influential?

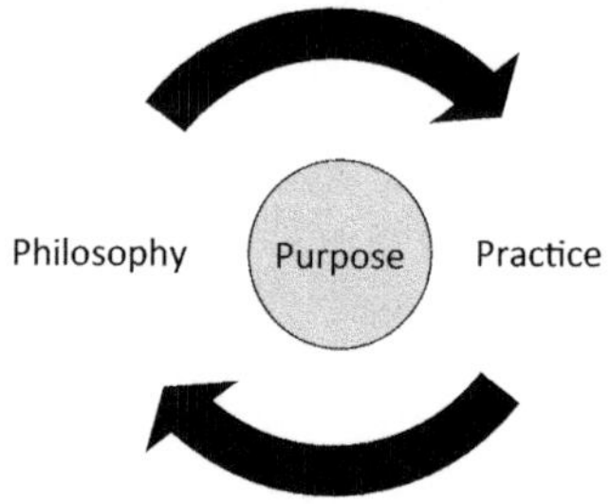

Figure 4.2 The 3Ps.

You may find this question easier to answer after reading Part Five – *do dialogue*.

As a leadership development professional, how did this section shape your leadership and learning philosophies and what, if anything, will you do differently in the future?

References

1. Plato (2010). *The Last Days of Socrates* (C. Rowe, translation). Penguin Books.
2. Weststrate, N.M. (2019). The Mirror of Wisdom. In: R.J. Sternberg & J. Gluck [Eds.]. *The Cambridge Handbook of Wisdom*. Cambridge.
3. Oakes, H., Brienza, J.P., Elnakouri, A., & Grossman, I. (2019). Wise Reasoning: Converging Evidence for the Psychology of Sound Judgment. In: R.J. Sternberg & J. Gluck [Eds.]. *The Cambridge Handbook of Wisdom*. Cambridge.
4. Oakes, H., Brienza, J.P., Elnakouri, A., & Grossman, I. (2019). Wise Reasoning: Converging Evidence for the Psychology of Sound Judgment. In: R.J. Sternberg & J. Gluck [Eds.]. *The Cambridge Handbook of Wisdom*. Cambridge.
5. Mickler, C. & Staudinger, U.M. (2008). Personal Wisdom: Validation and Age-related Differences of a Performance Measure. *Psychology and Aging, 23(4)*, 787–799.
6. Gluck, J. (2019). The Development of Wisdom during Adulthood. In: R.J. Sternberg & J. Gluck [Eds.]. *The Cambridge Handbook of Wisdom*. Cambridge.
7. William Shakespeare, As You Like It, Act V Scene 1, Cited in Aczel, B. (2019). Low Levels of Wisdom. In: R.J. Sternberg & J. Gluck [Eds.]. *The Cambridge Handbook of Wisdom*. Cambridge.
8. Edmondson, R. & Woerner, M.H. (2019). Sociocultural Foundations of Wisdom. In: R.J. Sternberg & J. Gluck [Eds.]. *The Cambridge Handbook of Wisdom*. Cambridge.
9. Oakes, H., Brienza, J.P., Elnakouri, A., & Grossman, I. (2019). Wise Reasoning: Converging Evidence for the Psychology of Sound Judgment. In: R.J. Sternberg & J. Gluck [Eds.]. *The Cambridge Handbook of Wisdom*. Cambridge.
10. Lawrence, P. (2021). *Coaching Systemically. Five Ways of Thinking About Systems*. Routledge.
11. Kotter, J.P. (1995). Leading Change: Why Transformation Efforts Fail. *Harvard Business Review, 73*, 59–67.
12. https://www.businesstoday.in/magazine/focus/story/meaning-of-the-word-facipulate-22742-2011-06–24
13. Oakes, H., Brienza, J.P., Elnakouri, A., & Grossman, I. (2019). Wise Reasoning: Converging Evidence for the Psychology of Sound Judgment. In: R.J. Sternberg & J. Gluck [Eds.]. *The Cambridge Handbook of Wisdom*. Cambridge.
14. Senge, P.M. (1990). *The Fifth Discipline*. Random House and Senge, P.M., Kleiner, A., Roberts, C., Ross, R.B., & Smith, B.J. (1994). *The Fifth Discipline Fieldbook. Currency.*
15. Lane, D.C. & Jackson, M.C. (1994). Only Connect! An Annotated Bibliography Reflecting the Breadth and Diversity of Systems Thinking. *Systems Research, 12(3)*, 217–228.
16. Lane, D.C. (1993). With a Little Help From our Friends: How Third-Generation Systems Dynamics and Issue-Structuring Techniques of 'Soft' or Can Learn

from Each Other. In: E. Zepada & J.A.D. Machuca [Eds.] *Systems Dynamics.* Systems Dynamic Society.

17. Lawrence, P. (2015). *Leading Change. How Successful Leaders Approach Change Management.* Kogan Page.
18. For example: https://www.theguardian.com/australia-news/2020/mar/21/bondi-beach-closed-down-after-crowds-defy-ban-on-gatherings-of-more-than-500-people https://www.smh.com.au/politics/federal/unacceptable-health-minister-blasts-beachgoers-amid-coronavirus-crisis-20200321-p54chw.html https://www.9news.com.au/health/local-council-warns-beachgoersoff-bondi/714872d5-e107-44f8-bbcd-a8c8e10eaa27
19. https://www.manhattanbeach.gov/Home/Components/News/News/4731/
20. For example: https://www.theguardian.com/world/2020/jun/25/major-incident-declared-as-people-flock-to-england-south-coast https://www.pedestrian.tv/news/bournemouth-beach-pandemic/ https://www.transportxtra.com/publications/parking-review/news/65975/major-incident-declared-after-thousands-flock-to-dorset-beaches/
21. Gluck, J. (2019). The Development of Wisdom during Adulthood. In: R.J. Sternberg & J. Gluck [Eds.]. *The Cambridge Handbook of Wisdom.* Cambridge.

Part Five

Do Dialogue

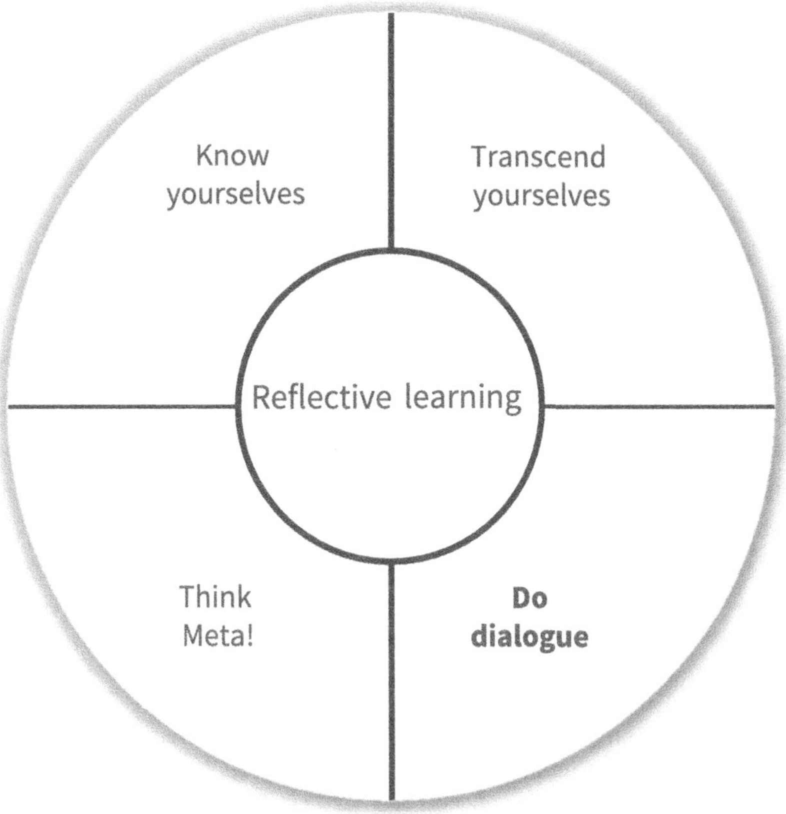

DOI: 10.4324/9781003284826-6

A leadership myth

Great Leaders Just Need to Engage in 'Active Listening'

Emma and her team sat down to review what to do next. They were responsible for the provision of IT services to staff across the organization, including IT infrastructure, laptops, helpdesk, and so on. Last week, working with their longstanding partner, they closed down services on Sunday morning to run an upgrade to client-facing systems. This required a lot of planning, since these days many people in the business, and clients, worked seven days a week. The upgrade had not gone well. It was scheduled to have been completed by noon, but the team was still trying to get it to work at 3 pm. In the end, they had to give up, abandon the upgrade, and regroup to decide when to reattempt the work. Emma got the team together to work out what had gone wrong and what to do next. She was concerned that the meeting could easily degenerate into finger-pointing and so asked everyone to listen to each other's points of view – to practice 'active listening' as she called it.

The conversation began:

Emma: Hiromi, what's your perspective on what happened?

Hiromi: Jane's team let us down. They manage the partner, and the partner failed us. They said the system was ready to install and it clearly wasn't. They've admitted that.

Jane: That's not entirely fair. It's true that they should have told us more about the risk of pressing the button on installation, but they were under a lot of time pressure because Hiromi's team were late in getting them the data they needed.

Hiromi: We were under time pressure because other departments were slow in getting us the information we needed. But the bottom line is, they said the system was ready to go when it wasn't.

Jane: I think your team could have done a better job in letting the business know what was going on. This is now a huge issue because we didn't warn anyone that there was a problem. If your team were finding it hard to collate the data, then you should have flagged the risk, rather than just expect the partner to manage to a much shorter time frame.

Hiromi: That's not my job, that's Emma's job.

Emma: OK, let's just take a time out. How well are well doing at listening to each other, real active listening?

Hiromi: I think we're doing fine. I've heard Jane acknowledge that the partner should have told us about the risk before implementing the installation. And she said my team should have alerted the business to what was going on, which actually isn't our responsibility.

Emma looked around the table. Everyone was leaning forward, fully alert and listening hard. But the meeting wasn't going well.

Theory

So far in this book, we have encouraged you to get to know your selves better and to develop an enhanced ability to transcend those selves in order to meet people where they are. To transcend ourselves requires thinking differently, a way of thinking that impacts how we conceive change and go about our work of leading change. Through the meta lens, the wise leader recognizes the impossibility of controlling outcomes. Change emerges from the multitude of interactions that take place throughout a social network. The role of the leader becomes to understand and appreciate the operation of that social network and to positively *influence* change.

In Part Five we will talk about dialogue. We think about dialogue as wisdom-in-action. In Part Four we talked a lot about how wise leaders think. In Part Five we will talk about what that thinking looks like in action as we encourage you to *do dialogue*. We'll explain in detail what we mean by 'dialogue' a little later, but first let's review some insights from the wisdom literature. The wisdom literature has more to say about empathy than it does about dialogue per se. Empathy shows up in lots of wisdom models, including the MORE Life Experience Model we referred to previously[1]. The capacity to empathize helps us to deal better with new challenges because it enables us to better understand how others are feeling[2]. We see mention of dialogical thinking, which is defined as the ability to see things from the perspectives of others[3,4,5]. The Berlin Wisdom Model identifies two practices that help people activate their wisdom[6]. The first practice is internal dialogue, as we advocated for in Part Two, in terms of helping your different selves get to know each other better and to learn to dance together. The second practice is external dialogue. In Part Five we will spend less time on dialogical *thinking* and more on the practice of dialogue – the *doing*. Doing dialogue is not easy because it requires us to think differently. That will become evident as we explore in this section what we mean by dialogue.

Doing dialogue may or may not require us to engage in active listening, that rather depends on what we mean by active listening. When we ask people what they mean by active listening, they either look unsure or talk generally about paying more attention. The phrase active listening has become too vague to be useful. Carl Rogers described active listening in terms of:

> "If I can listen to what he can tell me, if I can understand how it seems to him; if I can see its personal meaning for him, if I can sense the emotional flavour which it has for him, then I will be releasing potent forces of change in him."[7]

This is a demanding version of listening that requires the listener to attain a deep level of understanding of the other person. Contrast this definition with that of Thomas Gordon, a clinical psychologist, and colleague of Rogers:

> "Active listening is certainly not complex. Listeners need only restate, in their own language, their impression of the expression of the sender."[8]

Jo Tyler searched the term 'active listening' on Google and found most definitions to be highly transactional, relatively undemanding, and unambitious[9]. In this section we will share our own typology of listening. Whether you use our model or someone else's model, what is important is you are purposeful in your listening and have some typology to refer to help you be purposeful.

We will also talk about voicing. When we talk about engaging more effectively, and leading more wisely, we tend to focus only on listening and less on what we say. What we say is as important as what we hear in seeking to build trust. So, in this section, we will talk about effective voicing as well as listening.

How does the wise leader influence others? What does wise leadership in action look like in action? In this section, we invite you to consider how you currently lead and seek to influence and how you might experiment with different approaches to influencing. We encourage you to be even more purposeful about how you personally engage with others, and to think about what other conversations need to happen around you. Part Five is about what wise leadership looks like in practice. It addresses some of the fundamental basics of human communication that many leaders either dismiss, or assume they are already doing well. If we really aspire to become wise in our leadership, we need to revisit these 'fundamentals' and recognize how much more work we still have to do.

1 Dialogue

First, let's define what we mean by dialogue. We wrote the '*Tao of Dialogue*'[10] because we kept seeing people's eyes glaze over when we talked about the significance of dialogue. *Dialogue is just two people talking together, right?* – is what some people think – *we do that all the time.* Actually, no, that's not how we're using the word dialogue. We are defining dialogue as a particular type of conversation in which we choose to *suspend* our strongly held views in service of exploring new possibilities. Few people engage in dialogue at work. Most people spend most of their time engaged in monologue – either

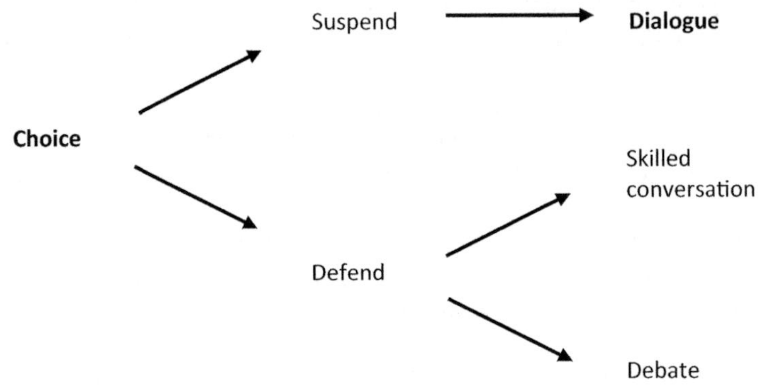

Figure 5.1 Dialogue (after William Isaacs).

i) debate, or ii) skilled conversation. Either way, they are invested, wittingly or otherwise, in defending a position rather than truly trying to hear and see the other person (Figure 5.1). Let us explore this idea further.

Organizations *are* conversations. Think about some of the most successful companies in the world. Hewlett Packard, for example, emerged from conversations in a garage in Palo Alto, San Francisco, conversations between Bill Hewlett and David Packard. Rumors have it that the 1996 merger of BP and Mobil European operations was born in a conversation between the leaders of both organizations when they found themselves sitting next to each other in an aeroplane. Organizations emerge from conversations through which people see what might be possible. New possibilities are more likely to emerge when people connect through dialogue.

When people engage in dialogue, they genuinely open themselves up to each other's ideas and perspectives, allowing room for new, unforeseen, ideas to emerge. Many new ventures fail. People agree to work together, but those people never truly align as to what will happen next. They haven't engaged in dialogue, rather they have made assumptions about what the other person thinks without testing those assumptions. Imagine what might be possible were we all able to move beyond everyday conversations and engage in genuine dialogue together. If we were able to suspend our beliefs and values and allow room for new perspectives and possibilities to emerge. As we have seen throughout this book, we are all connected to each other through a complex web of conversations and relationships. Our very identities are co-created with others through conversation. To lead change wisely requires us to embrace that connectivity, to look more deeply at ourselves and others. To listen and to voice and to be open to new perspectives. The better we *do dialogue*, the more able we are to cultivate new possibilities, to nurture the emergence of new possibilities from those with whom we engage. This ability is wisdom in action. So, in service of becoming wise leaders, let's unpack this deceptively simple idea of dialogue further. First, let's refer back to Figure 5.1

and spend a bit more time reflecting on the differences between debate, skilled conversation, and dialogue.

a) Debate

When we engage in debate, we are focussed solely on expressing our perspective, listening only to the other's perspective long enough to check whether they agree or disagree. Many leaders tend to gravitate toward debate. They spend much of their time in 'telling' mode, especially when time is precious. They are very busy, focused on being efficient and productive, striving to keep conversations concise and to the point. We know when we are in debate mode when we find ourselves focused on explaining and on ensuring the other person understands, ready to close off the other person going down a rabbit hole, quick to correct the person when they 'get it wrong'. When we find ourselves in this mindset then we are engaged in a form of monologue. In wondering how to *communicate better* we focus on clarifying our message and making it more compelling.

Debate is sometimes useful. If two people hold quite different views then engaging in a debate can help crystallize the key points that each person is trying to make and test those points, seeing to what extent those points appear to be well-reasoned and robust. Sometimes though, a debate is not helpful. Debate is rarely enough in working out how to move forward effectively in the face of complexity. Debate tends to be competitive. When people engage in debate you don't often see one of the participants stop and reflect thoughtfully that the other person might have a good point. If we over-privilege the value of debate, then we encourage people to think in competition. We encourage people to think in black-and-white. We encourage people to come up with logical, rational arguments, and to attach themselves firmly to a particular perspective on cause and effect.

Think of Brexit, for example. If you were following events in the UK at the time, you will have heard people expressing their views on whether to remain part of the European Union (EU) or not. Those who believed the UK should exit the EU expressed their views with absolute certainty. Those who believed the UK should remain part of the EU expressed their views with equal certainty. This debate might have been useful had the British people fully explored the claims being made by people on either side. The claim, for example, that trade with the EU would be tariff-free and involve minimal bureaucracy, claims that the Northern Ireland border would be 'absolutely unchanged', claims that Britain would take back control of its fisheries, that an extra £350m would be spent on the NHS and so on[11]. Claims from Remainers included that the UK would face an immediate £30bn hole in its finances. The debate was useful in terms of highlighting some of these assumptions, but the continuation of that debate rendered those insights relatively value-less. The Leavers and Remainers showed little interest in exploring the validity of their assumptions, instead focussing solely on attacking the assumptions of the other group. The conversation remained competitive. No one changed their mind. No one acknowledged the limitations of their own arguments. The Leavers failed to persuade the Remainers and the Remainers failed to persuade the Leavers. Instead, battle lines were drawn, reinforced, and levels of tension and anxiety across the country steadily grew.

There are times when this focus on monologue is appropriate and helpful. But being good at monologue won't, by itself, help a leader to navigate complex change successfully.

b) Skilled conversation

Debate is an obvious form of a monologue. Skilled conversation is less obviously monologic. When engaged in skilled conversation people do listen to each other's perspectives, seek to understand those perspectives and acknowledge them. The purpose of the conversation is to find an outcome both people can live with. The extent to which people are prepared to give way on some issues though is limited. Certain beliefs and opinions are non-negotiable. Every participant seeks to identify a way forward that doesn't offend others' non-negotiables. What emerges from the conversation is likely to be some form of compromise.

Skilled conversation might be usefully regarded as expert negotiation. There is clearly a role for skilled conversation in change. Indeed, many change agendas may be negotiated satisfactorily solely through people's capacity to engage in skilled conversation. But there will be times when skilled conversation isn't enough. For example, when approaching complex problems, when no one is entirely sure what is going on now, let alone what changed state they ought to aspire toward. Complexity often demands the emergence of something new and original, something outside the experience of those conversing. But generating something new is unlikely to happen while people remain firmly attached to their non-negotiables.

c) Dialogue

What might have happened in the UK had Leavers and Remainers put aside their convictions for a while and focused only on imagining a new future, a future within or without the EU? What might have happened had people declared themselves neutral, committed only to generating something new and different? It's hard to imagine people like Nigel Farage, Boris Johnson, and Michael Gove engaging in such a conversation. Boris Johnson reportedly spent a weekend writing two articles for the Daily Telegraph, early in

2016, one advocating Leave and the other Remain. At the end of the weekend, he submitted his arguments in favour of leaving and stuck to that decision thereafter. Notice the individualist binary thinking. He didn't focus on outcomes or invite conversation around different ways of achieving those outcomes.

We don't engage in dialogue often. If we are not genuinely purposeful in how we choose to engage, then most of us are subject to our deeply held beliefs and opinions. If someone says something we disagree with, then our attention is directed inward, to querying what we have just heard, telling ourselves why that perspective is wrong, and wondering how we will respond. We are quick to assume we understand what people are telling us and go into reactive mode. To engage in dialogue is to *suspend*, as depicted in Figure 5.1. When we engage in debate or skilled conversations, we take non-negotiables into the conversation, parameters that limit the potential of that conversation. Some of those non-negotiables are clear to us, and we may be explicit about them. Others, our more general deeply held beliefs and opinions, we may be less aware of. We call these non-negotiables our '*noble certainties*' and we must be aware of and be able to *suspend* our noble certainties if we are to get better at doing dialogue.

What do we mean by our 'noble certainties?' William Isaacs called our deeply held beliefs and opinions our 'noble certainties'[12]. These noble certainties often take the form of judgments, and these judgments, often unconscious, get in the way of our ability to do dialogue. So, the extent to which we can engage in dialogue depends on the extent to which we are aware of our noble certainties, and the extent to which we can listen beyond those noble certainties. For example, Emma and her team are still arguing about who is to blame for the failed IT upgrade.

Hiromi: You should have told the business that the upgrade wasn't going to be delivered on time.

Emma: I didn't know what was going on. How can I keep the business informed if you don't keep me informed?

Hiromi: I sent you an e-mail.

Emma: I'm not always on e-mail. When something's really important or urgent, you need to call me.

Hiromi: When we're delivering a key project, I think it's up to you to be monitoring progress, keeping us all together, and to be reading your emails.

Emma: You need to take more accountability than that.

This is debate. Hiromi is stuck on a noble certainty that says:

> "Leaders are accountable for making sure they know what is going on."

Emma is stuck in a noble certainty that says:

"Everyone is responsible for staying in touch and letting others know what is happening."

Neither is invested in seeking to understand each other's perspectives. The conversation has become a competition, with each focussed solely on attacking the other person's argument and defending their own. As it stands, they are unlikely to agree. Nor are they likely to come up with something brand new. Sometimes people do manage to negotiate their way to a solution. This is 'skilled conversation':

Hiromi: You should have told the business that the upgrade wasn't going to be delivered on time.
Emma: I am of course responsible for the overall performance of the team, Hiromi, but we all have our different roles to play. I believe it's up to all of us to keep each other informed.
Hiromi: I sent you an e-mail.
Emma: I appreciate that, Hiromi, but when we're working on a project as important as this one, then you need to be sure that I have received the message.
Hiromi: Do you not think that when we're working on an important project you need to be readily available?
Emma: I think that's a fair point Hiromi. I will, from now on, make a point of paying close attention to my emails, and I would ask you to call me, not just email me.
Hiromi: I can agree to that.

This feels like a better outcome. Yet still, neither Hiromi nor Emma has let go of their noble certainties. They have skilfully worked around their differences without insulting each other or the conversation breaking down. The solution they have come up with may be a good one, but it may not be the best solution. What might happen if they both suspend their noble certainties and just focus initially on listening respectfully to the other?

Hiromi: You should have told the business that the upgrade wasn't going to be delivered on time.
Emma: You see it as my job as leader to know what going on at all times, regardless?
Hiromi: I think so.
Emma: Then when we have a super-important project like this one, what should I be doing?

Hiromi: Well, I don't want you standing over my shoulder. That would be annoying. I think what's bothering me is that you didn't read my email. If the project is that important, I would have thought you would have been glued to your inbox.

Emma: I think I had a different mental model in my head. I thought if something important was going on, then you would call me, not email me. So, I didn't even have my inbox open. But I was walking around with my phone in my hand.

Hiromi: We seem to be focussing only on the communication between us two. Should we be communicating by phone or email? But what everyone else?

Emma: What are you thinking?

Hiromi: I'm wondering if we should use a team app that allows everyone to be telling everyone else what's going on, so that anyone on the team can quickly understand where the whole project is at any point in time.

When we engage in dialogue, suspending our noble certainties (or our judgements), then new possibilities often emerge. Common noble certainties that get in the way of this type of conversation include:

- I already know the best answer to this problem
- I'm the expert on (whatever the subject is)
- I know exactly what you're talking about

To engage effectively in dialogue requires that we are aware of our noble certainties and that we manage them. Think back to a recent conversation that didn't go well.

- What were your noble certainties?
- Which of your selves held those noble certainties?
- Which of your selves is best at persuading all your other selves to suspend their noble certainties?

We can think about our capacity to engage in dialogue in terms of how we listen *and* how we speak. Let us consider each in turn.

a) Purposeful listening

Earlier we said that we didn't think 'active listening' was a very useful construct and that we would share a different listening typology. This typology describes five ways of listening. Each has its place, but if we are not purposeful and choiceful, we may revert to an ineffective way of listening in some scenarios, particularly those scenarios that demand us to be curious. The five ways of listening are (Figure 5.2):

i) Listening for gaps

When we listen for gaps, we listen to see if others are speaking. We are not listening to what they are saying, we are just listening for the opportunity to jump in with what we have to say without being seen to interrupt. We are listening intently because we don't want to be seen as being rude. We are listening intently to the tone of the person speaking and the pace at which they are speaking, trying to anticipate when we can step in and say our bit. We are listening intently to the thoughts in our head, saying things like '*when will she be quiet!*' and '*would he mind if I interrupted now?*' This is sometimes an effective way to listen, for example when my sole purpose is to convey a message without offending rules of social etiquette. Often it is not.

ii) Listening to words

Listening to words is what most of us do, most of the time. When we listen to words, we are listening to the words and adding our own meaning to those words, wittingly or not. We are anticipating what we think others will say and assuming we understand without checking in to make sure. For example, when my friend says, '*I hope the weather works out this weekend*,' I assume she wants the sun to shine so she can go to the beach. Actually, she wants it to rain because the plants are dying in her backyard. When my colleague says '*I wish my manager would coach me more often*' I assume she wishes her manager would encourage her to think through issues for herself. In fact, she wishes her manager would tell her what to do because she hates making decisions herself.

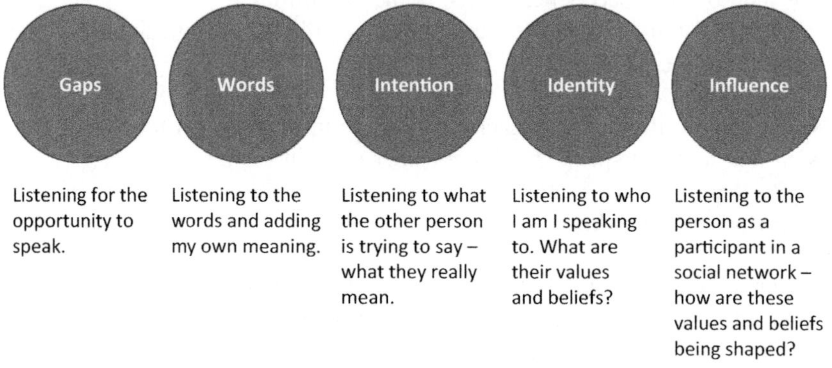

Figure 5.2 Five ways to listen.

When we listen only to words, we are liable to make assumptions and jump to conclusions. When we listen to words, we may be listening intently. We can recite back every word the other person said. We are still listening intently also to the voices in our head, the voices assuring us they know what the other person is trying to say. We're working through issues in our heads, looking for solutions, and quickly sifting through what others are saying – does it make sense? – does it not make sense? – making assumptions along the way. Again, don't dismiss the value of this form of listening. If I'm in a hurry, working with people who I know well, when the decisions we are making are low value, and low risk, then this form of listening may be perfectly appropriate. But it's not a form of listening likely to help us lead change.

iii) Listening to intention

When we listen to intention, we make a conscious effort to understand what the other person is trying to say. This isn't easy. As Krishnamurti, an Indian philosopher once said[12]:

> "If we try to listen, we find it extraordinarily difficult, because we are always projecting our opinions and ideas, our prejudices, our background, our inclinations, our impulses; when they dominate we hardly listen at all to what is being said."

When we are listening for intention, we are constantly checking in with the other person. Not because we have been taught to paraphrase, but because we are curious; we want to know if we have really understood what the other person is trying to say. If we are truly seeking to understand the other person, then the voice in our head will be saying things like 'do I really get it?' and 'does that mean what I think it means?' We will find ourselves asking questions without thinking about it, seeking to clarify and understand. We will find ourselves reflecting and summarising. When we listen for intention, we don't sit passively – we engage.

iv) Listening to identity

When we listen for identity, we are listening for the person. We may have already understood what they are trying to say, but that doesn't mean we have fully understood why that person believes what they seem to believe. When listening for identity I get curious as to why the other person looks at the world the way they do as well as how they look at the world the way they do. When we listen for identity, we seek to understand the person – who is this person? What are we learning about their values, motivations, and life experiences? What are we learning about the way they see the world?

By listening for identity, we get to know people better. Consider the following exchange:

Hiromi: You should have told the business that the upgrade wasn't going to be delivered on time.

Emma: You see it as my job as leader to know what going on at all times, regardless?

Hiromi: I think so.

Emma: That's what you expect from a good leader; that they are always available. That they are anticipating what may go wrong in your area and are always there to support you?

Hiromi: Something like that, yes. The leader is responsible for the effort of the whole team, not just their own deliverables. The leader isn't afraid to roll up their sleeves and get their hands dirty. Everyone in the team has the opportunity to get to know the leader and understand what they are thinking. The leader role models the hard work that's sometimes required to get things done.

What values and beliefs do you think you detect in Hiromi? Emma thinks she is hearing some things about hierarchy, hard work, and collaboration. She'll need to ask more questions to further explore how Hiromi is thinking, but just by asking a couple of questions she already feels she understands Hiromi a lot better.

To listen for identity requires energy. It requires tuning out of content, resisting the temptation to attend only to the matter at hand. It requires that we tune into disagreement, because through understanding our points of disagreement we can develop a better understanding of each other. How often do we do that though? – tune into disagreement rather than get sucked into defending our view or debating?

v) Listening for influence

The first four ways of listening encourage us to think individualistically, to regard others as autonomous and discrete. When listening for identity I get curious as to why the other person looks at the world the way they do as well as how they look at the world the way they do. We all make meaning together. We are social in our meaning-making. When we listen to others, and who they are as people, we can go a step further and wonder with whom they have been making meaning? Who else has played a role in this person showing up as I experience them to be?

The fifth way of listening is based on the idea that who we are (our identity) is fluid and dynamic and is constantly being shaped through our interactions with others. This idea is consistent with both the complex and meta-systemic ways of thinking. The complex systemic lens will direct us specially to consider the influence of others within a 'system' or sub-system' – the individual's team or division or organization for example. The meta-systemic perspective encourages us to think more broadly. Consider the following exchange:

Emma: I'm getting a sense that role is important to you, that senior managers should take personal responsibility for the performance of everyone in the team?

Hiromi: Y-e-es.

Emma: Why do you think that's so important to you?

Hiromi: Partly my culture. That's how I was brought up, but that's how I've worked in the past. My previous bosses were all like that too.

Emma: When you say a cultural thing …

Hiromi: I mean that's how things were in my family and in my country. My father was quite strict with us, and he worked in a company where people were expected to do what their bosses told them to do.

Emma: And you worked yourself in some company cultures that were like that too.

Hiromi: Not the same, but bosses did tightly manage the actions of their direct reports.

Listening for influence is particularly useful when seeking to influence change across an organization. Your efforts to persuade the organization person-by-person are unlikely to succeed. Each of those people is in conversation with lots of other people too. If you want to persuade the masses, you may need to engage the masses in the same conversation.

These five ways of listening offer us a language through which we can be much more specific as to how we choose to listen in any given situation. If I wish to listen for identity, for example, because I believe I need to get to know this person better given their role in the organization, then I will listen for the person's beliefs and values. I won't be listening for the opportunity to express my opinion. I won't be listening only to the words the person is speaking, but also to their intentions, and the underlying personas expressing those intentions.

Purposeful listening helps us to build stronger relationships with others. When we listen for words, or even for intentions, it is easy to react from our own sense of right or wrong. If, for example, someone gives me feedback, disrespectful feedback, complaining that I never deliver my work on time, or that I don't pay attention to other people's feelings, I may find myself drawn into defending myself. I protest. If I'm listening for identity or for influence, then I am curious as to where this feedback is coming from. I stay curious. I want to understand what event is being referred to and how the other person made sense of that event. This helps me to respond on the basis of a deeper understanding of the other person and their needs.

b) Respectful voicing

You may have come across various models we are supposed to use when giving others feedback. These models ask us to distinguish between how we are feeling about an event in the moment, and what actually happened. For example, I feel the need to tell my colleague how badly they let me down by not turning up to a meeting. The SBI model, invented by the Center for Creative Leadership, encourages us to deliver our feedback in three chunks:

Situation	It took me three weeks to get the client to agree to this meeting. I was relying on you to be there to share your expertise.
Behaviour	You didn't show up.
Impact	The client felt the meeting was a waste of time. I think we may lose their business.

People are encouraged to speak from the 'I', to avoid labelling people (e.g., *'you clearly couldn't care less about what others are trying to achieve – you're so not a team player!'*). When we label people, we attack people, which usually elicits defensive behaviour, and our conversation quickly becomes a debate.

These models are useful, but we need to go further if we wish to become wiser. In saying what we feel needs to be said, we don't just need to speak from the 'I' – we need to *think* from the 'I'. If we think from the 'I' then whatever we say will be respectful and is likely to be well received. If we speak from the 'I' but are still thinking in judgmental terms, then our emotions leak out. Whatever we say is still likely to elicit defensive behaviours and endanger the relationship.

To *think* from the 'I' requires us to be selves-aware, aware of the inner voices that are filling our head with thoughts, often judgmental thoughts. It requires us to transcend our vociferous selves and to be curious about the world through the other's eyes (selves-transcendence) and it requires us to respect others' values and beliefs as well as our own values and beliefs (by thinking meta!). In short, it requires us to be respectful – to create space for the other person and their perspective on the world.

To find that respectful space requires us to move to identify and move beyond our noble certainties, which usually requires some full-on emotional management, another aspect of selves awareness we talked about in Part Two. The wisdom literature tells us that wise leaders are sensitive to the feelings of others, and to their own emotions. They pay attention to those emotions and are good at managing, or regulating, those emotions. Wise people are viewed as calm, patient, serene, and emotionally controlled[13]. Wise leaders can say what needs to be said, without labelling people or voicing judgment, and while staying calm.

2 Dialogue and change

Having spent some time on dialogue let us loop back to make clear the links between dialogue and change. In the research behind '*Leading Change. How Successful Leaders Approach Change Management*'[14] we interviewed 50 leaders around the world, asking them to tell us stories about change and what they did to successfully deliver change. These leaders told us stories about being open and transparent, telling stories, giving feedback, and crafting messages to address people's concerns. These leaders framed communication as a two-way process, a process of listening *and* voicing, a process through which new ideas emerged and people connected with each other. Several leaders spoke about a personal journey in coming to recognize the importance of dialogue vs. monologue.

> "I myself needed to go through a personal change journey. I needed to learn to shut up and listen. I had to be less aggressive. You get to leadership because you know the answers. You need to transition to asking questions, and it's not a transition everyone makes well. I recognised it was a journey that I needed to make."

These leaders described a two-way communication process. For example, the Vice-President of a medium-sized retailer.

> "With one or two colleagues I explained the change to every retail business in each state and explained it personally. What and why. Authentically and open. It made me accessible so they could understand, and I gained an understanding of what their concerns were so that I could hear and respond."

From the stories, we deduced that change emerges from dialogue and that great leaders do dialogue well. This might be intentional dialogue initiated in service of change, or it might be unplanned dialogue from which change emerges anyway. Conversations take place all over an organization, all the time. The role of the leader is not to try and force a message through – an approach that rarely works, rather the role of the leader is to influence, to engage in the conversation, listening and voicing, always with respect. To encourage dialogue and reflective learning, often in the moment. The leaders we spoke to understood communication to be a social meaning-making process. The abilities of the leader to understand others' perspectives, to tailor the message to an audience, and to assess issues in a non-judgemental fashion, were all core to their stories. They all recognized the need to create time and space for people to engage with change on their own terms, and to acknowledge their own role in seeking to understand how others related to change. There was a general and explicit acknowledgement that top-down linear approaches to change were usually ineffective.

The wise leader then, isn't just good at dialogue. The wise leader recognizes the significance of dialogue in enabling change at the organizational level. The wise leader doesn't just engage in lots of one-to-one dialogue, but engages also in group dialogue, and thinks about who else needs to be engaged in dialogue and when. The wise leader doesn't think about dialogue in simplistic terms. She knows that dialogue is hard and that she needs to have a close eye on power dynamics.

Power dynamics

People often ask us – I'm trying to do dialogue, but no one wants to do dialogue with me. David Bohm was one of the first people to write about dialogue and he voiced a rather pessimistic perspective[15]. He wrote:

> "There is no place in the dialogue for the principle of authority and hierarchy. Rather, we need a place where there is no authority, no hierarchy, where there is no special purpose – sort of an empty place, where we can let anything be talked about."

But all organizations are, to an extent, hierarchical, and different people have different levels of authority. We cannot pretend that they don't. When two people meet to discuss an issue, there is always a dynamic going on in the room and an important aspect of that dynamic is power. This doesn't mean there is no point in trying to engage in dialogue. As Bohm says, *'you can have a dialogue in a more limited way, perhaps with a purpose or goal in mind'*.

When we talk about power, we think straightaway about positional power. If five people are engaged in conversation and one of them is the other's boss, this inevitably impacts the dynamic. Everyone knows that the boss has ultimate decision-making authority. That likely limits the extent to which people feel comfortable sharing their perspectives and bestows upon the leader a privileged role in deciding what will be heard and what won't. That doesn't mean that aspiring to dialogue isn't useful. We ought to be aware of the pitfalls of thinking about dialogue and other forms of conversation in binary terms.

In considering the power dynamics of the conversations in which you participate, don't limit yourself to a consideration of positional power. There are other forms of power. For example:

- If you have been working in your organization for longer than others in your group, and you have a broader network of internal colleagues then you may have more network power. In which case your views may be more likely to shape the conversation.

- if you have more extensive networks outside the organization then you have a different form of network power and again your views are more likely to predominate.
- If you have more technical expertise relevant to the conversation, then your expert power may be most influential.
- If you have access to resources that no one else has access to, you have power.
- If you are quite fierce, and excellent at debating, you may have a form of personal power.

We tend to think straightaway of positional power, and the need to engage people higher up the organization. We might dust down the organization chart and use that as a basis for understanding how power operates in the organization, but if we consider only positional power, then our hypotheses as to how the social network is operating are unlikely to serve us well.

In the book '*Leading Change*'[16] we came across various real examples of power in action. For example, expert power. This leader spoke about the implementation of a new system.

> "The system was built in the late nineties and was the core system for the entire business unit. It was developed in-house and just a handful of people remained who knew how it worked. It was a handcuff for the business because it was old and problematic. It was difficult to make changes and some enhancements had to be made to the system due to regulatory changes. We decided to replace the legacy system with an outsourced system, piggy-backing a competitor system, but there was a lot of resistance to even broaching the idea. The legacy system experts picked on functionality that couldn't be replicated and held it up as deal-breakers, or they didn't come to meetings, or they bad-mouthed the executive and the competitor's system. But we needed them until post-migration. So, we offered them money to stay even though their behaviour was poor. They had power."

Other sources of power include resource and network power. An organization moves office.

> "The new office was to be open plan without exception. Lots of people actively fought to retain their offices and we had to ask the CEO to ring people up to tell them they weren't going to get an office. All except the funds managers. They were key, even more important than the CEO. We had to compromise with them. We lost that battle."

This story is about relational power:

"When I went to the global head office, I didn't read it well. I had a team of three and wanted to get them to work together better. I misread the politics; people have their own agendas and interests. My predecessor wasn't strong and his 2IC (second-in-command), now my 2IC, had taken over. The 2IC wasn't interested in changing the way we worked; he was just interested in maintaining his relationship with the Vice President, and the Vice President didn't want to piss off the 2IC because he was giving him what he wanted. It took me a while to realise the 2IC had no interest in my success and no interest in supporting the change. I found myself unable to do the job I'd been brought in to do; the VP always asked my 2IC to come to meetings. I learned that you've got to make sure you know how everyone is linked to the stakeholders, and that you understand the lines of authority and how they work."

The wise leader, thinking meta-systemically, is attuned to these different forms of power and is guided in her efforts to lead change by these insights. In any complex project, there are multiple power dynamics at play, dynamics that are dynamic and volatile. The wise leader observes relationships in action in her efforts to work out how the network is operating in-the-moment.

So, in suggesting you *do dialogue*, we don't suggest you try and *do dialogue* all the time. We suggest that you build on your capacity to *think meta!* leveraging your selves-awareness and ability to selves-transcend, by enhancing your capacity to engage in dialogue when dialogue is useful. We encourage you to spend time working out how you believe the organization really works, and where dialogue may be missing. In working out how the organization works you will need to consider the various power dynamics within your organization and take those dynamics into account when deciding what type of conversation you want to engage in with who.

Epilogue

Emma and the Team Do Dialogue

Emma and her team talk about the purposeful listening model and decide to focus on listening for intention, listening for identity, and listening for influence. Emma asks the team to be patient with each other, to allow plenty of time for enquiry and listening before coming to conclusions as to what went wrong and what they need to do to ensure a successful upgrade.

Emma: Hiromi, what's your perspective on what happened?

Hiromi: I have some insights as to what happened, but right now I have more questions than conclusions. My first question is around what happened in the partner team? It's my understanding that the partner said the system was ready to install, whereas it seems it wasn't. I'd like to understand better what happened there.

Jane: I have spoken to them about that. They have put their hand up and said that one of the team made a mistake. It seems he got stressed out, afraid what would happen if the upgrade went wrong, and launched the installation without having fully considered the risk.

Hiromi: Can you tell us more about the person who made the mistake?

Jane: I don't know how senior he was. I'm still finding out exactly what happened. I'm more curious about their protocols and how it was he was able to launch the installation without some form of risk assessment taking place, at least a conversation. But I don't have the full story yet.

Emma: Why was he so stressed?

Jane: They got a lot of the data late. It meant they were really rushed, but still believed they had to meet the deadline.

Emma: What might we have done differently?

Jane: Well (looking at Hiromi), I think we must acknowledge that we delivered them the data late, and somewhere along the line we need to understand why at least some people on their team thought the deadline was immovable, no matter what.

Hiromi: The data was late. We had problems getting the data from some internal departments.

Emma: So, we received the data late, we passed it on to them late. They felt obliged to hit the deadline anyway, and then things went wrong.

Jane: Yes.

Emma: What compounded it all was that we didn't succeed in keeping the business up to date with progress.

Hiromi: I don't understand what happened there, Emma. I sent you several emails, telling you we were having problems gathering the data?

Emma: OK. Sorry. I wasn't even looking at emails. I just assumed we'd call each other if things weren't going well.

Jane: Sounds like we need to agree around the communications piece before we try again with the upgrade.

Hiromi: Agreed.

Self-development

In Part Five then, we offer guidance in becoming better at dialogue. First, we would remind you that dialogue is not only about our capacity to listen. It is also about our capacity to express ourselves whenever we feel obliged to make comment, and to do so respectfully. Here are five areas you may choose to focus on. Consider these reflective questions.

1 Listen purposefully

In Part Five we outlined the purposeful listening model. With reference to that model:

1 When do you find yourself engaging in each of the five ways of listening – in what contexts?
2 Which of your selves are present in those contexts? Which of your selves are particularly good at listening for intention and listening for identity?
3 How would you *like* to be listening in each of those contexts? Which of your selves might you call upon in those situations?
4 How will you be more purposeful in your listening, moving forward?

2 Voice respectfully

In Part Five we talked about respect. Respect means being able to manage your inner voices, to head judgment off at the pass, to be curious about other people's experience of an event. It likely requires you to manage your emotions. To manage your emotions better requires that you understand the emotionality of each of your different selves. For each of your selves, ask:

- What scenarios trigger unhelpful emotions?
- On the basis that thoughts drive emotions, what automatic thoughts are triggered in the moment that lead to those emotions?
- How would you challenge those emotions?

For example, Action Shaun is triggered when people don't deliver what they promise to deliver, thereby slowing Action Shaun down. He gets angry and on occasion sends an email to the person concerned, an email he later regrets. Shaun thinks about the last time this happened. He felt he was let down by Gert, a colleague. He recalls the following thoughts-in-the-moment:

- Gert doesn't care
- He's left me in the lurch
- This isn't the first time
- I can't trust him
- I'm going to get into trouble now
- I'm going to have to stay late

Shaun makes the time to reflect and challenges those automatic thoughts. He decides:

- Gert seems to be a reasonably caring person
- I *am* going to have to work a bit harder to get the job done on time
- He did this once before, but he usually does what he says he will do
- I don't know why he didn't deliver the work on time

Shifting the thoughts shifts the emotions. Action Shaun may still feel some annoyance, but the level of annoyance is likely to be less than it was, sufficiently diminished that he is unlikely to send rude emails. And we see some curiosity emerging, a desire to understand more about what happened. This curiosity makes it more likely Shaun will succeed in engaging in an exploratory dialogue. You may also choose to reflect again on those initial thoughts. What values and beliefs do they suggest? This is an opportunity to learn more about your selves.

Reflecting now on your voicing – how often do you say what needs to be said? How often do you stay silent?

1 When you choose to say what needs to be said, how often do you do so respectfully?
2 What else do you need to do to enhance your capacity to say what needs to be said respectfully?
3 Which of your selves might you bring forth to ensure that what you say is respectful?

3 Identify your noble certainties

We said that to engage in dialogue requires that we manage our 'noble certainties'. These are those beliefs and convictions that get in the way of my listening. We listed five common noble certainties:

- I already know the best answer to this problem
- I am closer to this issue than you are
- I know the people involved better than you do
- I'm the expert on (whatever the subject is)
- I know exactly what you're talking about

These noble certainties get in the way of our listening. Consider:

> It's Friday and one of your team tells you they must leave early, which means they won't get the report they promised you today, until next Monday. This team member is twenty years younger than you. She always has entertaining stories to tell on a Monday about what she got up to the previous Friday night. She often fails to get her reports in quite on time – she often needs an extra couple of hours to achieve a deadline. She looks perfectly healthy to you right now and has swapped her flat shoes for heels.

In thinking about what to say next, what noble certainties might you be experiencing? For example:

- Integrity is important and integrity is about doing what you say you'll do. This person lacks integrity because she doesn't often deliver her work on time
- Leaving work early without having completed all your work is unprofessional unless you're sick
- This is a young, single, woman who is more interested in meeting up with her friends for drinks than doing a good job at work

To what extent do you make time to reflect on those noble certainties, in service of being curious and respectful? If am to listen independently of my noble certainties, first I must identify them, and then I must challenge them. I challenge them and hear my selves saying:

- I don't know why she wants to leave early
- It's possible to enjoy a good social life and be committed to your work
- I haven't yet made the time to give her feedback on her report writing. Nor have I enquired as to why she sometimes submits her reports late. I shouldn't assume she doesn't care.

The reflective process shifts me from feeling frustrated and judgemental, to calm and curious, and respectful.

Think about a real scenario, a conversation you engaged in recently that could have gone better. Ask yourself the following questions:

1 What noble certainties played out?
2 What triggered each of those noble certainties?

3 Which of your multiple selves sat behind each of those noble certainties?
4 What could you have said to those selves to suspend each of their noble certainties?

4 Make time for reflective learning

To engage in dialogue is hard. It requires us to be selves-aware, to be able to selves-transcend, and think meta! This is hard stuff, and to get better at dialogue requires us to make the effort before, during, and after conversations to prepare and learn from our attempts. If we don't make the time for reflective learning, then we will find our selves locked into the same old patterns of engagement. We have suggested some questions you might ask yourself – when will you make time to ask yourself those questions? Who will you engage in that reflection with? To what extent are you committed to engaging in reflective learning while in the midst of conversation?

5 What about everyone else?

Every time we take a group through the mechanics and value of dialogue someone says something along the lines of, *'It takes two to tango, right? I might want to engage in dialogue, but how do I make the other person engage in dialogue too?'* This is a great question. The straightforward answer to this question is – you can't *make* someone engage in dialogue, but you may be able to influence them. Here are some thoughts:

a **Role model.** If you show up deeply curious and intent on understanding the world through another's eyes, this will probably feel strange to the other person. It's not often that someone genuinely seeks to understand what we are thinking and feeling, especially in a fast-paced work environment. That person will likely feel listened to in a way they rarely feel listened to. They will likely sense that you are genuinely interested and curious and will probably feel less anxious about being heard. The more they feel understood the more likely they are to start asking you questions, about what you are thinking and feeling. That may not happen in the first conversation, or the second conversation, but will happen as that person comes to believe that you have their interests at heart.
b **Adopt a common language.** We often work with teams, introducing them to the idea and benefits of dialogue. Once everyone in the room has a shared understanding of what dialogue is, how it can be helpful, and when, then you have a shared language. You can explicitly agree when to engage in dialogue and can hold each to account during the conversation, to give each other the best chance of staying in dialogue.
c **Dialogue as aspiration.** Some commentators say that dialogue is impossible within an organization. No matter the subject, they say, people will be

coming to the conversation with different agendas, at least parts of which they will remain committed to pushing through. Those with the most power are able to steer the conversation where they want it to go. Those with less power will be thinking hard about how to be best heard, which may mean 'weasel wording' rather than 'respectful voicing'. We don't disagree with these sentiments; indeed, we have already declared that pure dialogue is impossible since it demands absolute selves-awareness. But we don't think any of that matters. It's not always helpful to be thinking we are either in dialogue or we're not. Dialogue may be best thought of as aspirational, and the more often we are able to create moments of dialogue, however fleeting, the more able we will collectively become at managing complexity and uncertainty.

Designing interventions

In Parts One to Four we focussed on who your leaders are, recognizing that leaders exist at every level of an organization. We looked at their commitment to reflective learning, their commitment to better understand who they are, their commitment to transcend those selves, and their capacity to think meta. In Part Five we look at what leaders actually do. The essential task of a leader is to influence, and to effectively influence the leader leads to be able to engage in effective conversation. In Part Five we offer you further thoughts to build on.

1 Dialogue sits at the heart of leadership

As we have said before, the essential task of any leader at any level is to effect change, and change is navigated through conversation. Whether it be an early in career leader faced with the task of giving feedback to a direct report, or a more experienced leader seeking to manage a large corporate merger, that leader's capacity to achieve desired outcomes will be enhanced by their ability to engage in effective conversation. They understand the different types of conversation and are proficient in engaging in each of those kinds of conversation. Dialogue is perhaps the most challenging kind of conversation, because of the effort it takes to suspend our noble certainties and create a respectful space, and because it demands high levels of selves-awareness. If everyone in your organisation understood dialogue and was good at dialogue, then your organisation would be more successful. This is an argument for building dialogue into multiple programs. Build your feedback training around principles of dialogue. Build your coaching programs around principles of dialogue. Include dialogue in building sophisticated programs on diversity and inclusion. The more people have been introduced to the principles of dialogue, the easier it becomes for everyone to engage with each other. The easier it is to contract around engaging in dialogue and to hold each other to account.

2 Start at either end and make it practical

If your people understand principles of *selves-awareness, transcendence of selves,* and *think meta,* then they will be ready to embrace the notion of dialogue. On the other hand, you can introduce people to the principles of dialogue without working through those materials first. You may choose to start people's journeys toward greater wisdom from either end of the five mantras.

Whether your people have been introduced to the other four mantras or not, we suggest you make your sessions practical. When you bring your people together, face-to-face, or virtually, minimise the time you spend explaining the theory and maximize the time you spend reflecting on theory and giving it a go. Create and allow as much time as possible for people to make sense together. The theories and frameworks of dialogue are relatively simple and straightforward to understand. You can convey those theories in short, concise pre-reads, and post-reads. In our experience, most people grasp the theory relatively easily. They find it much more challenging putting those ideas into practice. For example, people generally find the principles of purposeful listening easy to understand, but when it comes to putting them into practice, some people really struggle. They slip quickly into giving advice and telling people what to do. They find it hard to resist fixing stuff. Moreover, they often know they are struggling, yet still find it hard. Hence the importance of making your sessions practical, ensuring people have access to feedback on their efforts, and the time to reflect on those efforts. If you teach dialogue only as a concept, you are unlikely to see much behavioural change in your organization.

Providing people with the opportunity to practice, receive feedback, and process that feedback, is essential. Most organizations build such opportunities into their programs somewhere, but often the time allotted is curtailed. We are so keen to explain all our wonderful models that somehow the practice, feedback, and reflection time gets squeezed.

If your people have already been introduced to the other four mantras, then these practice sessions provide further opportunities to reflect on the operation of different selves and the capacity of the individual to transcend those selves. If your people haven't been introduced to the other four mantras yet, then we certainly recommend that you frame a conversation around a commitment to reflective learning, and that you take the opportunity to introduce the idea of selves-awareness – if it feels appropriate to do so.

3 Leverage group coaching

Again. As we said, people tend to understand these ideas conceptually but struggle to put them into practice. The group is a wonderful opportunity to make sense of the materials, to give it a go with each other, to receive feedback, to make sense of the results of our efforts. The world has become incredibly fast-moving at the same time as it has become more complex.

People are working hard and getting overly tired. They are getting conditioned to working environments that demand of them the ability to get things done quickly. To engage in dialogue requires slowing down and committing to a process of co-reflection. And there is lots to reflect upon – *selves-awareness*, our capacity to *transcend those selves*, and our determination to create with others the time to have a different kind of conversation. The group is a wonderful opportunity for people to support each other in their efforts to do dialogue back out there in the workplace. It's a place again to make sense of the materials, design experiments, and to learn together from the outcomes of all our experiments.

4 Go l-o-n-g and support reflection

Again. We evaluate our programs over time and have found that whilst many people understand principles of dialogue quite quickly and say that they are putting those principles into practice, when we talk to the people with whom they interact we hear a different story. Through the eyes and ears of those with whom these people work, it can take six months before they start to feel a real difference in the way people relate to them. It takes six months before participants feel that these new ways of thinking and these new behaviours become part of their normal way of doing things. Up until that point they remain as 'interesting behaviours that I never have time to put into practice'. Those interesting behaviours become ingrained only with the opportunity to be held to account for behaving differently and the opportunity to reflect with others in the organization about what works and doesn't work.

Your 3Ps revisited

Let's look one more time at the 3Ps (Figure 5.3).

As a leader, what ideas have resonated for you in this section? For example, the idea that:

- Active listening is too vague a term to be useful
- The five ways of listening may be more useful
- That all ways of listening are good, but some are better than others in some contexts. We need to be deliberate and purposeful else risk endangering important relationships
- We need to say what needs to be said and do so respectfully. To speak with respect means being good at emotional management
- To lead change effectively means being good at dialogue

How did our suggestions for self-development resonate with you in terms of getting better at dialogue? What will you make a conscious effort to do differently? How will you stay on track – how will you link these efforts to your efforts to engage in more effective reflective learning?

As a leadership development professional, how did this section shape your leadership and learning philosophies and what, if anything, will you do differently in the future?

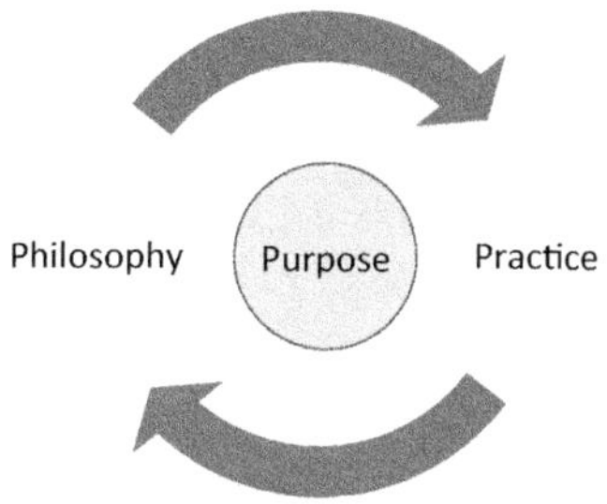

Figure 5.3 The 3Ps.

References

1. Gluck, J. & Bluck, S. (2013). The MORE Life Experience Model: A Theory of the Development of Personal Wisdom. In: M. Ferrari & N. Weststrate [Eds.]. *The Scientific Study of Personal Wisdom*. Dordrecht.
2. Hursthouse, R. (2006). *Practical Wisdom: A Mundane Account*. Proceedings of the Aristotelian Philosophy.
3. Ferrari, M. & Kim, J. (2019). Educating for Wisdom. In: R.J. Sternberg & J. Gluck [Eds.]. *The Cambridge Handbook of Wisdom*. Cambridge.
4. Sternberg, R.J. & Hagen, E.S. (2019). Teaching for Wisdom. In: R.J. Sternberg & J. Gluck [Eds.]. *The Cambridge Handbook of Wisdom*. Cambridge.
5. Levenson, M.R., Jennings, P.A., Aldwin, C.A., & Shiraishi, R.W. (2005). Self-Transcendence: Conceptualization and Measurement. *International Journal of Aging and Human Development*, *60*, 127–143.
6. Stange, A. & Kunzmann, U. (2008). Fostering Wisdom: A Psychological Perspective. In: M. Ferrari & G. Potworoski [Eds.]. *Teaching for Wisdom*. Springer.
7. Rogers, C.R. (1961). *On Becoming a Person*. Houghton Mifflin.
8. Gordon, T. (1977). *Leader Effectiveness Training*. Wyden books.
9. Tyler, J. (2011). Reclaiming Rare Listening as a Means of Organizational Re-enchantment. *Journal of Organizational Change Management*, *24*(*1*), 143–157.
10. Lawrence, P., Hill, S., Priestland, A., Forrestal, C., Rommerts, Hyslop, I., & Manning, M. (2019). *The Tao of Dialogue*. Routledge.
11. https://www.politico.eu/article/15-things-uk-vote-leave-promised-on-brexit-and-what-it-got/
12. Isaacs, W. (1999). *Dialogue: The Art of Thinking Together*. Doubleday.
13. Weststrate, N.M., Bluck, S., & Gluck, J. (2019). Wisdom of the Crowd: Exploring People's Conception of Wisdom. In: R.J. Sternberg & J. Gluck [Eds.]. *The Cambridge Handbook of Wisdom*. Cambridge.
14. Lawrence, P. (2015). *Leading Change. How Successful Leaders Approach Change Management*. Kogan Page.
15. Bohm, D. (1996). *On Dialogue*. Routledge (page 49).
16. Lawrence, P. (2015). *Leading Change. How Successful Leaders Approach Change Management*. Kogan Page.

Conclusions

In the introduction, we said that we need to change the way we think about leadership. We need new paradigms and new approaches to developing leaders. We have looked to the world of wisdom for inspiration and found what we believe to be a highly practical and new approach to leadership.

Definitions of wisdom include reference to intelligence and empathy and to traits such as life experience, humility, self-awareness, openness to change, propensity to reflect, a positive mindset, comfort with ambiguity, commitment to learning, and a desire to serve the common good. As we immersed ourselves in the wisdom literature, so the five mantras emerged, five themes that seemed to capture all these elements in a leadership framework. The mantra *know yourselves* includes a reference to self-awareness. The mantra *transcend yourselves* guides us to new ways of thinking that necessarily invoke humility, comfort with ambiguity, and a desire to serve the common good. *Think meta!* translates that way of thinking into the organizational context and the challenge facing all leaders – how to lead change? *Do dialogue* provides practical guidance on how to go about acting wise. And at the heart of the five mantras sits a commitment to *reflective learning*. Wise leaders are curious, open to change, and find positive pathways in their reflection upon life experience, good or bad.

As we wrote *The Wise Leader* the five mantras came to feel increasingly connected. Wisdom, we feel, starts with an exploration of self. The multiplicity perspective offers a richer, more sophisticated understanding of self. It isn't enough, however, to understand who I am. I need to understand how I am in relation to others, I need to explore the possibility that who I am is constantly evolving through my relationship with others. This transcendental perspective requires us to think quite differently, and this shift in how we think, it is argued, is developmental. We then remind ourselves that there are multiple perspectives on wisdom, and we are reminded by the wisdom literature that it may be most meaningful to frame our depiction of wisdom with context in mind. The *Think Meta!* mantra builds on the idea of self-transcendence and paints a picture as to what self-transcendence might look like in someone leading change. This leads us to consider *Do Dialogue*, which

DOI: 10.4324/9781003284826-7

is effectively self-transcendence in action from a leader's perspective. We have been sharing our thinking around dialogue with leaders for years. Different people have made their own sense of dialogue; some have embraced the idea, others found it uninteresting, and others made their own personal sense of the materials, perhaps in line with our thinking, perhaps not. In writing the book we see the connections between selves-awareness, transcendence, and dialogue – to be great at dialogue requires us to do the work on selves.

The journey toward wisdom then is never-ending in that none of us will ever be completely selves-aware, or achieve total selves-transcendence, but some of us get further than others, and some of us get there faster. We ended up placing the commitment to reflective learning in the middle of the five mantras because we believe that this commitment is what enables some people to move steadily toward greater wisdom, while others – however much experience they accrue – seem to make much less progress.

Our purpose in writing this book has been to frame the challenge as clearly as we can, drawing on wisdom from the wisdom literature, and providing our best guidance as to how you might approach the next steps of your journey. To progress on that journey requires not only a commitment to reflective learning, but also giving your selves permission to challenge conventional wisdoms around leadership and leadership development. We have in this book challenged ideas such as:

- Intelligence and empathy are all you need to be a great leader
- We can become wiser by focusing only on what we do and not how we think
- To reflect more often necessarily leads to becoming wiser
- Authenticity is about gaining a better understanding of our one true self
- We can control change
- We enhance our relationships with others through 'active listening'
- Organizations are systems
- Leadership development is an individual endeavour
- Churning whole populations through cookie-cutter short programs will lead to enhanced leadership capacity

Wisdom is developmental. It requires us to access new, fundamentally different, ways of *thinking* about the world. If we think differently then we will act differently. If we want our leaders to behave differently, if we have strong beliefs around achieving pragmatic, practical outcomes, we won't see those outcomes realized without paying attention to how people think.

The wisdom literature tells us we don't become wiser by trying to become wiser. We become wiser by becoming more purposeful in the way we live our lives and by actively reflecting on our endeavours to achieve our purposes. Wise leaders are purposeful, and they are engaged in a continual process of reflective learning; they reflect while doing as well as before and after doing. We need to design leadership programs to support this process.

If this all sounds daunting, then we encourage you to think multiple. Instead of holding up wisdom as something perfect and therefore unattainable, consider the idea that all of us are wise in some respects. Go looking for the wisdom you already embody and for the wisdom in others. If you don't believe anyone is wise, then you will have no one to learn from. That belief may make the whole idea of wisdom rather unhelpful.

Finally, we remind you that there is no single definition of wisdom, and that many wisdom theorists believe we must devise our own models of wisdom that best suit our professions and the cultures we work within. We encourage you to continue playing with your 3Ps (Philosophy, Purpose, and Practice). Your 3Ps will inevitably continue to evolve and change if you are a reflective learner. You may consider finding a group of like-minded people, and committing to grow together with those people, supporting each other on your journeys to greater wisdom.

Whatever sense you made of this book; we hope it was worth your time. Good luck, and stay in touch with Paul at www.leadingsystemically.com and Suzi at www.roarpeople.com.au.

Index

For Product Safety Concerns and Information please contact our EU representative GPSR@taylorandfrancis.com Taylor & Francis Verlag GmbH, Kaufingerstraße 24, 80331 München, Germany

Batch number: 09019466

Printed by Printforce, the Netherlands